Accession no.
36187063

KU-534-480

Doing Your
PGCE at M-Level

Education at SAGE

SAGE is a leading international publisher of journals, books, and electronic media for academic, educational, and professional markets.

Our education publishing includes:

- accessible and comprehensive texts for aspiring education professionals and practitioners looking to further their careers through continuing professional development

- inspirational advice and guidance for the classroom

- authoritative state of the art reference from the leading authors in the field

Find out more at: **www.sagepub.co.uk/education**

Doing Your PGCE at M-Level

SECOND EDITION

A GUIDE FOR STUDENTS

EDITED BY Keira Sewell

LIS - LIBRARY

Date	Fund
22/9/15	Snr-xe

Order No.

2657247

University of Chester

Los Angeles | London | New Delhi
Singapore | Washington DC

© Keira Sewell, Liz Lakin, Alex Woodgate-Jones, Tim Cain, Kate Domaille 2012

First published 2008
Reprinted 2008, 2009 and 2010
Second edition 2012

Apart from any fair dealing for the purposes of research or private study,
or criticism or review, as permitted under the Copyright, Designs and
Patents Act, 1988, this publication may be reproduced, stored or
transmitted in any form, or by any means, only with the prior
permission in writing of the publishers, or in the case of reprographic
reproduction, in accordance with the terms of licences issued by
the Copyright Licensing Agency. Enquiries concerning reproduction
outside those terms should be sent to the publishers.

SAGE Publications Ltd
1 Oliver's Yard
55 City Road
London EC1Y 1SP

SAGE Publications Inc.
2455 Teller Road
Thousand Oaks, California 91320

SAGE Publications India Pvt Ltd
B 1/I 1 Mohan Cooperative Industrial Area
Mathura Road
New Delhi 110 044

SAGE Publications Asia-Pacific Pte Ltd
3 Church Street
#10-04 Samsung Hub
Singapore 049483

Library of Congress Control Number: 2011935748

British Library Cataloguing in Publication data
A catalogue record for this book is available from the British Library

ISBN 978-1-4462-0829-8
ISBN 978-1-4462-0830-4 (pbk)

Typeset by Kestrel Data, Exeter, Devon
Printed in Great Britain by MPG Books Group, Bodmin, Cornwall
Printed on paper from sustainable resources

CONTENTS

About the Authors

Keira Sewell has worked in teacher education and Initial Teacher Education for over twenty years and was the Primary PGCE course leader from 2006 to 2010. She now leads Visionary Education Consultancy (http://www.visionary-education.co.uk), specialising in support for teachers and trainees and quality assurance and strategic management in schools, higher education institutions and companies. She is particularly interested in the role of the integration of theory, research and practice in the developing professional.

Tim Cain is Professor in Education at Edge Hill University. He has research interests in mentoring, music education, action research and initial teacher education.

Kate Domaille was Secondary PGCE course leader at the University of Southampton from 2002 to 2010. She now works as an independent consultant supporting a range of education projects in higher education and schools, focused around teacher training and continued professional development. (Contact: kate.domaille@btinternet.com.)

Liz Lakin is Lecturer in Life Sciences at the University of Dundee, with specific responsibility for Schools' Liaison. Her research interests focus on teaching and learning in the Biological and Environmental Sciences and areas of pedagogic expertise include developing and enhancing independent learning.

Alex Woodgate-Jones is a lecturer on the Primary PGCE programme at the University of Southampton. She is particularly interested in the role of reflection and the relationship between research, theory and practice.

List of Figures and Tables

Figures

Tables

List of Abbreviations

ADHD	Attention Deficit Hyperactivity Disorder
BERA	British Educational Research Association
CEDP	Career Entry Development Profile
CPD	Continuing Professional Development
DfEE	Department for Education and Employment
EAL	English as an Additional Language
FHEQ	Framework for Higher Education Qualifications
GCSE	General Certificate in Secondary Education
GTCE	General Teaching Council for England
HEFCE	Higher Education Funding Council for England
iGCSE	International General Certificate of Secondary Education
ICT	Information and Communication Technology
INSET	In-Service Training
ITE	Initial Teacher Education
IWB	Interactive Whiteboard
KS	Key Stage
LSDA	Learning Skills and Development Agency
MFL	Modern Foreign Language
NALDIC	National Association for Language Development in the Curriculum
NPQH	National Professional Qualification for Headship
PGCE	Postgraduate Certificate in Education /Professional Graduate Certificate in Education
PGDE	Professional Graduate Diploma in Education (Scotland)
PSHE	Personal, Social and Health Education
QAA	Quality Assurance Agency
QCA	Qualifications and Curriculum Authority
QTS	Qualified Teacher Status
SBT	School-Based Training
SKU	Subject Knowledge and Understanding
TDA	Training and Development Agency for Schools
UCET	Universities Council for the Education of Teachers
VAK	Visual, Auditory and Kinaesthetic

Introduction

We write this second edition of *Doing Your PGCE at M-Level* at a time of great change in education. Although we are used to such change, I cannot remember a time when so much has been completely up in the air at the same time. We face changes to the ways in which teachers are trained and the role of higher education institutions in this, changes to the curriculum and qualifications, changes to assessment and changes to the bodies and organizations which will monitor and regulate all of these. While this may appear to be an unsettling time, what it does do is reinforce the view that we reiterate throughout this book: that teachers must have the skills, the knowledge and understanding, the ability to think critically about education and, above all, the willingness not only to embrace new thinking but to initiate it.

There are so many routes into teaching now that it is difficult to identify which one is the best for your particular situation. If you already have a degree, it is unlikely that you would be willing to spend another three or four years on an undergraduate teacher training programme and, therefore, the postgraduate programmes will present the most attractive option. In the past, you would have only had one route – the PGCE. This was a well-established award which everyone understood to identify someone who has completed an undergraduate degree at honours level and then gone on to do a one-year full-time equivalent course to learn how to be a teacher. Changes in initial teacher education, brought about through the introduction of the Professional Standards for Qualified Teacher Status, and changes in academic awards, brought about through changes in the National Qualifications Framework, specifically the Framework for Higher Education Qualifications (FHEQ), have meant that the PGCE is no longer quite so easily recognizable. Nowadays, the PGCE is no longer confined to one year of study, sometimes taking 18 months or even two years, and the outcome could be one of two awards, the Postgraduate Certificate in Education or the Professional Graduate Certificate in Education, both of which normally carry with them recommendation for Qualified Teacher Status (QTS). Of course, you could also learn to be a teacher through an employment-based route which may have no academic award but does lead to QTS, but that would be another book altogether. This book aims to guide you through what doing a PGCE at M-level actually means both in terms of study and in terms of your future career as a teacher.

All the authors who have contributed to this book have had extensive experience in designing and delivering PGCE programmes, and many of us were involved in the development of the very first Postgraduate Certificate in Education programmes in 2004: the PGCE at M-level. As a result, we have been able to listen carefully to students' questions and issues around this route into teaching and have seen some of the problems they face. We have used case studies and examples drawn from our own experiences and practice and it is our hope that this guide will answer some of the questions you may have, from choosing which route to apply for to gaining employment and continuing your studies.

As tutors on established PGCE M-level programmes we often get asked questions which relate to the structure and requirements of the programme. These include questions like: 'Do I have to do the M-level assignments?' 'Will the PGCE M-level be harder than the PGCE H-level?' It is, therefore, very important that you understand the differences between the two awards and how they came about. In Chapter 1 Liz Lakin and I explain this with the aim of helping you decide which route to apply for, or, if you are already on one of the routes, whether to take up the option offered to you by your institution to transfer to the other route. Its contents will help you prepare for the selection process at your chosen institution by explaining the differences between the two and it will help you to understand why your programme is structured and organized in a particular way. By exploring these areas, this chapter will help you to understand the relationship between academic study and school-based practice in both the Postgraduate and the Professional Certificate routes.

One of the common perceptions of students when they first start the PGCE M-level is that the M-levelness of the programme is confined to the assignments and the lectures or seminars which underpin these. Chapters 2 to 5 aim to firmly establish the idea the M-levelness will permeate through all aspects of your programme, from the taught sessions in all subjects or in professional themes to your work in schools. In Chapter 2, Liz Lakin begins this by exploring the role of M-level study at subject level. Personal development of subject knowledge and understanding is explored alongside the ways in which research and theory support your development as a subject specialist. The relationship between learning and teaching and your own role within both of these processes is an integral part of this chapter and will help you to recognize the approaches available to you both as a learner and as a teacher.

In Chapter 3, Alex Woodgate-Jones examines how M-level study supports the development of the critically reflective teacher. She explores the definition of 'reflection' and encourages you to take on responsibility for your own development as a professional. In this chapter you will be encouraged to consider how reflective practice can enable you to move forward and reflect on how you can best work with your mentor during your school-based training.

The role of research in teaching is an integral one and one which enhances our practice. Tim Cain explores this relationship in Chapter 4, highlighting the importance of trustworthy and valuable research in the development of educational theory. He uses the development of learning theories to exemplify this relationship and to analyse the impact of such research on current educational practice. In this chapter you will also be introduced to approaches to reading research and encouraged to think about the different ways research is presented to us. Finally you will be introduced to the ways in which you can research your own practice, taking account of such things as the types of research available to you, the development of research questions and selection of research methods, and data collection techniques and the ways in which data is analysed and presented. This chapter will also direct you to reading which will further support your development as a researcher in education.

Writing assignments and doing academic work at Masters level is often a major concern for students on the PGCE at M-level. 'What does Masters level writing look like?' 'How is it different from what I did in my first degree?' 'How does doing an assignment make me a better teacher?' All are questions commonly heard echoing around initial teacher training institutions that offer the PGCE at M-level. In Chapter 5, Kate Domaille explores these questions using theoretical examples and real case studies.

One of the challenges yet to be fully addressed with regard to the PGCE at M-level is getting employers to recognize it as different from the PGCE at H-level and to understand the benefits brought by students who have chosen this route into teaching. Chapter 6 explores the ways in which you can use the knowledge, skills and attributes developed through study at Masters level to secure your first teaching post. Advice is given on how to structure letters of application which make a potential employer want to read on and place you on the shortlist, and this advice continues to support you through the rest of the selection process, from planning a sample lesson to answering questions from a panel of interviewers.

Although, having completed the PGCE, you may decide that you have had enough of study for the time being, Chapter 7 explores the ways in which you can continue your studies. It introduces the range of options available and invites you to consider what appeals to you personally. Although I recognize that there are many potential barriers to continuing your studies, this chapter also offers practical solutions which may help to reduce, if not completely remove, these barriers.

Our aim is that this book will be a constant companion throughout your time on the PGCE and will help to answer some of the questions you may have. While no one can claim that the PGCE, either M-level or H-level, is easy, we hope that you will find the challenge it offers enjoyable and that this guide will support you during your time on the PGCE. If you are reading this you are on the first stages of entering the best profession in the world where no two days are the same and where your impact on pupils will be lifelong and sometimes life-changing. Welcome to the profession.

Keira Sewell

1 What will the PGCE at M-level do for me?

Keira Sewell and Liz Lakin

This chapter aims to help you to understand the difference between a Postgraduate Certificate in Education and the Professional Graduate Certificate awards so that you can:

- decide which PGCE route you should apply for;

- decide whether to opt for the Masters module option once you have been accepted onto a PGCE programme.

What is the difference between the Postgraduate Certificate in Education and the Professional Graduate Certificate in Education?

In 2004, the Framework for Higher Education Qualifications (FHEQ) was brought into effect and this meant that institutions had to look at their range of awards to ensure that they fitted into the framework. PGCEs were a long-established route in initial teacher training and many understood that their role was to provide a professional qualification for those who already had a first degree. However, the term 'postgraduate' suggests that the academic work done will be at a higher level than that done in an honours award, whereas on most courses, this was not the case. This meant that Initial Teacher Education (ITE) providers needed to review their programmes to ensure that if they called their award postgraduate, it did indeed include academic work of a postgraduate nature, that is work at Masters level or level 7. Institutions were free to choose their own route; some decided to offer a Professional Graduate Certificate in Education in which the academic work would be at Honours level (H) or level 6, while others decided on the Postgraduate Certificate in Education route which included academic work at Masters (M) level (level 7). Both routes continued to lead to Qualified Teacher Status (QTS). Essentially, then, the difference between the two is the level at which you have to do the academic work: level 6 or 7.

What does a PGCE at M-level look like?

Perhaps surprisingly, there is no guidance on what the PGCE M-level or the PGCE H-level should look like beyond the requirements for QTS. This means that courses can differ greatly yet lead to the same award. When deciding which route to follow it is useful to look at the following three things: the award options, the structure and organization of the course, and the admissions requirements.

Award options

As stated above, in England there are two award outcomes to a taught postgraduate course of study leading to Qualified Teacher Status: the Professional Graduate Certificate in Education or the Postgraduate Certificate in Education. The only difference between the two is the level at which the academic work is done. Some institutions have elected to offer only one or the other, while others offer both. Where institutions offer both you may be required to enrol on one route and then, with guidance from your tutors, elect to move to the other. For example, in some institutions everyone enrols on the PGCE M-level, but if you gain lower grades in your assignments you may be awarded a Professional Graduate Certificate in Education. In other institutions you enrol on the PGCE H-level but if your academic work is considered of high quality you are encouraged to work for the Postgraduate Certificate in Education.

In the Scottish system things are slightly different in that postgraduate study for teacher training leads to a Professional Graduate Diploma in Education (PGDE), the details of which are discussed later in this chapter.

It is important to recognize that the Professional Graduate Certificate in Education is equivalent to the award you would previously have gained had you undertaken a PGCE at most initial teacher education institutions in England, Wales or Northern Ireland prior to the implementation of the FHEQ. It is important, therefore that this award is not seen as the 'deficit' model, but rather that the Postgraduate Certificate in Education is seen as the 'surplus' model.

The Professional Certificate in Education leads to the professional qualification of QTS and achievement is assessed through both academic work (usually practice-based assignments) at level 6 and demonstration of the competences outlined in the Professional Standards for QTS. The award of Postgraduate Certificate in Education requires academic study at postgraduate level, that is level 7, in addition to demonstration of competency against the standards for QTS. It is, however, important to understand that while the academic study is at M-level, the PGCE is not a Masters award. It can contribute to a Masters award if you choose to continue your studies following completion of the PGCE (see Chapter 6 for further detail on this), but it does not automatically lead to one. Whichever award you choose to follow, you will notice that the award title does not include 'QTS'. This is because institutions do not have the power to award QTS, only to recommend to the General Teaching Council for England (GTCE) that they award this. This is important, as the development of the FHEQ has enabled some separation of the academic and the professional awards, resulting in the range of routes now available for those wishing to teach. For example, the Graduate Teacher Programme route leads only to recommendation for QTS and does not carry with it an academic award. Some institutions have separated out the two elements of the PGCE so that it is possible to exit with a PGCE with QTS, just a PGCE or just QTS, although these cases are rare. This range of awards has led to some confusion in the teaching profession and it is important that you can explain your award to a potential employer when applying for your first teaching post. This is explored further in Chapter 6.

Structure and organization of the award

In terms of structure, it is useful to see the PGCE as having two elements: the academic element leading to a postgraduate or professional award which is governed by the institution, and the professional element leading to recommendation for QTS which is governed by the

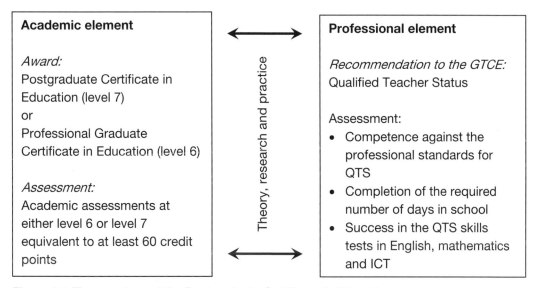

Figure 1.1 The structure of the Postgraduate Certificate in Education

Training and Development Agency for Schools (TDA). The key difference between the awards of Postgraduate Certificate and Professional Graduate Certificate is the level of the academic element, as the requirements for the professional element are the same in each. As Figure 1.1 shows, theory, research and practice link the two elements in both awards.

Let us first examine the academic award-bearing element of this structure. While the FHEQ outlines the exit criteria for a PGCE at M-level, it does not specify the number of credits which would lead to this award; neither does it specify a structure which all PGCEs must follow. As a result, different institutions organize this element in different ways. Most institutions have taken the guidance offered by the Universities Council for the Education of Teachers (UCET), the Training and Development Agency for Schools (TDA), the Quality Assurance Agency (QAA) and the Higher Education Funding Council for England (HEFCE), and consider the PGCE M-level equivalent to 60 credit points of study at level 7. This could be arranged as two modules, each of 30 credit points, or three modules each of 20 credit points, or some other combination that leads to a total of 60 credit points studied at level 7. One of your decisions should be how many assignments you want to do. Look at the programme specification for the PGCE at the institution of your choice, which will tell you how the modules are arranged and assessed. Some institutions have also elected to include level 6 credit points, often applying these to assessments designed to demonstrate competence in the Professional Standards. These could be credit points given to successful completion of school placements or assessments in specific subject areas. As a result, a PGCE could include up to 120 credit points, made up of both level 7 and level 6 work. Again, it is important to note that the number of credit points included within the PGCE will often be reflected in the number of assignments you are required to complete – those having 120 credit points sometimes require up to five assignments.

Not only does the number of credit points an institution applies to its PGCE vary, so too do the assessment strategies used. Some have written, theoretical assignments only, while others include small-scale research projects, presentations and critical evaluations of work undertaken in schools or even extracts from teaching practice files.

The professional element of the PGCE is governed by the Training and Development Agency for Schools (TDA), which has provided institutions with the statutory requirements of the Professional Standards for QTS and the Initial Teacher Education requirements which underpin these. At the time of writing these are under review but, whatever format they will take, they govern everything from what criteria are required for admission to a teacher training programme to how many days trainees must spend in school during their training. As a result, there will be more commonality between PGCEs in this element. For example, courses have to be structured so that students normally spend a minimum number of days in school (90 days for a primary course and 120 days for a secondary course); they have to complete the QTS Skills Tests in English, mathematics and information and communications technology; and they must be able to demonstrate competence against the Professional Standards for QTS for the age range they are being prepared to teach. There will be some variance in practice as institutions are free to decide how such things as the number of days in school are organized, how competence against the standards will be recorded and assessed, and the amount of time allocated to each subject area. For example, institutions may have two, three or even four placements, each in a different age phase (Key Stage 1 and 2 in primary, or Key Stage 3 and 4 and A level in secondary).

Depending on their locality, some institutions may also need to consider how certain competences can be effectively supported for trainees. For example, the demographic of partnerships between schools and teacher training institutions means that certain standards which require you to engage all pupils and personalize learning appropriately to meet the needs of individuals may be more wide ranging in some areas than in others. This is particularly pertinent when partnerships are largely with monolingual schools and trainees have less opportunity to develop their understanding of how best to support children for whom English is an additional language. In this case, trainees may need to meet this through focused work in short-term placements in specially selected schools which provide the opportunities and experiences necessary. You may wish to consider this when selecting your training institution.

In the PGCE M-level, perhaps the most important element is the way in which the course organization supports the level of study required and it is this area which has required institutions to think carefully about the ways in which this can be best achieved. While the M-level element of your PGCE will permeate through both your school-based and your university-based work, a premise explored in greater detail in the following chapters, there may be additional elements to a PGCE M-level programme which would not be evident in the PGCE H-level. These could include specific study skills sessions focusing on such aspects as writing in a critically reflective way, accessing and reading journal articles, using methods of referencing texts consistently, research methods, and data collection and analysis techniques. These may be offered as part of the taught programme but some institutions offer optional sessions either during the programme or during the summer vacation prior to entering the course. These are designed to recognize the fact that you all come with a range of backgrounds and it cannot be assumed that you will be able to write or conduct research in the manner required for this award.

Study at M-level requires autonomy, independence and time for reflection and many institutions will try to allow opportunities in the very hectic PGCE programme for you to develop these skills. There will be a requirement to carry out directed tasks or independent study, thus extending the actual time of the PGCE well beyond the structured, taught programme.

Admission requirements

The admissions requirements for both awards are very similar as most of these relate to the QTS element of the course. For application to both routes you need to provide evidence of a minimum of Grade C GCSE or equivalent qualifications in English, mathematics and science, qualification in a first degree (usually at honours level), experience of working with children, preferably in a school context and in the age range you wish to teach, and having met the requirements for physical and mental fitness to teach and have no criminal record which would bar you from working with children.

In the past, the only difference you may have encountered between the two routes was the classification of first degree, with the PGCE at M-level requiring a minimum degree classification of upper second class. However, recent developments in teacher education suggest that only those trainees with upper second class honours degrees will have access to funded places and the competition for places on initial teacher training means that first degree classification is becoming an important criterion for selection.

 Activity

Consider how your academic profile and your personal and professional experience to date prepare you to do a PGCE at M-level. How can you best communicate this to your chosen institution and what else could you do to enhance your personal profile in this increasingly competitive market? For example, would further voluntary work in a wider range of schools support your application?

How do I decide which route is for me?

The answer to this is very personal and therefore it is difficult to provide a generic response; however, it is useful to dispel a few misconceptions about the choice of route. The most common of these include the idea that doing the PGCE at M-level will entail more work; that this route will be much harder than doing the PGCE H-level; and that doing the PGCE at M-level adds little to the skills required for effective practice in the classroom. Let us explore these.

First, does the PGCE M-level really mean more work? In most cases, the PGCE M-level does not entail more work than the PGCE at level 6; indeed, it may even require less. In both routes you need to complete assignments, but in some institutions the M-level assignments have been devised in such a way that you actually do fewer, longer assignments than on the PGCE at level 6. For example, on a PGCE H-level you may need to do as many as five assignments, one on each of the core subjects (English, mathematics and science), a generic assignment on teaching and learning, and possibly an assignment on information and communications technology (ICT) or even a specialist subject. In the PGCE M-level you could do as little as two assignments. Therefore, it may be useful for you to decide whether you would rather do five shorter assignments or two longer ones.

Secondly, let us explore the idea that doing a PGCE at M-level is harder than doing it at H-level through the notion of challenge. All new learning presents challenge and it is in the level of challenge that the differences between the two routes become evident.

Let us go back to your first degree. In year 1 you were working at certificate level (level 4) on the FHEQ. After successfully completing year 1 you then progressed to year 2 where you were working at intermediate level (level 5). Following this you moved to year 3 (and sometimes year 4 depending on the structure of your degree) where you will have been working at honours level (level 6). At each stage you will have found the level of academic work a little more challenging and the criteria on which your work was assessed a little more detailed. You will have seen that, increasingly, you were required to be more critical, analytical and evaluative in your thinking; that you were required to develop a broader and deeper understanding of the body of knowledge in your first degree subject or focus; that your skills of communication were becoming more complex and that you were able to engage further in debate and support and justify these debates with reference to a wider range of literature; and that you were able to begin to challenge the arguments and assumptions put forward by others.

At the end of each level you were able to make the transition to the next as your skills in academic study and your knowledge of your subject or focus area were developing, often without you even realizing this was happening. This kind of development is normal in academic study and resides firmly in the premise that the more you practise something, the better you get at it. I remember being upset to find I had been graded 'D' in one of my first assignments, but on looking back now I realize that I had simply churned out the views (some of them very suspect ones) of other authors with no attempt to challenge them or suggest alternatives. I thought that all I had to do was string together lots of quotations to demonstrate that I had read a lot of books! Try this activity yourself:

 Activity

Read one of your assignments submitted in the first year (level C) of your degree. Now read one of your assignments from the final year of your degree (level H). Write down the things that you feel are different between the two pieces of work. Now see if you can determine where you learned to apply these different approaches.

The likelihood is that you cannot pinpoint the exact moment that you learned how to develop your skills in academic work, but rather that it was an ongoing process that developed throughout your first degree. This development will be the same in the PGCE at whatever level you choose to study but the extent of challenge will be different depending on the route chosen.

If you decide to do the PGCE at H-level, you will be required to take on another body of knowledge which is different from the one you took on in your first degree and, in this respect, this route will present challenge. However, in terms of academic skills, those of thinking in a critical, analytical and evaluative manner and communicating your debates in a style commensurate with this level of academic study, you will be working at a level which should be well within your comfort zone as it will be similar to the level you were working at in the final year of your first degree.

The PGCE M-level, however, will require you not only to take on another body of knowledge but also to make the next transition in terms of developing your academic skills. Let us have a look at what the FHEQ says about the differences between the two levels:

Honours level (Level 6)
An Honours graduate will have developed an understanding of a complex body of knowledge, some of it at the current boundaries of an academic discipline. Through this, the graduate will have developed analytical techniques and problem-solving skills that can be applied in many types of employment. The graduate will be able to evaluate evidence, arguments and assumptions, to reach sound judgements and to communicate effectively.

An Honours graduate should have the qualities needed for employment in situations requiring the exercise of personal responsibility and decision-making in complex and unpredictable circumstances.

Masters level (Level 7)
Much of the study undertaken at Masters level will have been at, or informed by, the forefront of an academic or professional discipline. Students will have shown originality in the application of knowledge, and they will understand how the boundaries of knowledge are advanced through research. They will be able to deal with complex issues both systematically and creatively, and they will show originality in tackling and solving problems.

They will have the qualities needed for employment in circumstances requiring sound judgement, personal responsibility and initiative in complex and unpredictable professional environments.

(QAA, 2001)

But what does this actually mean? What are the differences between the two? The key difference has two elements: a knowledge and understanding of teaching and learning; and the transferable skills which enable this to be put into practice. Let us first explore the former.

In terms of knowledge and understanding, H-level graduates would be expected to have an understanding of a *complex body of knowledge*, some of which may be at the *current boundaries* of education. At M-level this understanding will have been informed by current theory and research at the *forefront* of education. In other words, someone who leaves with a Postgraduate Certificate in Education will have an understanding of current thinking about some areas of education and will be prepared for teaching in the future as well as teaching in the present.

In terms of the skills and attributes developed, M-level work requires an ability to engage in critical analysis and evaluation of both current and emerging theory and research underpinning effective education, and to apply their thinking systematically and creatively when dealing with complex issues and problem-solving. M-level graduates are required to demonstrate originality of thought, something which requires them not only to look at how things are at the moment but to consider how our developing understanding can inform future practice. They are self-directed and act with autonomy when planning and implementing tasks at a professional or equivalent level. Through the synthesis of their developing knowledge and understanding of education and their ability to think deeply and critically they are required to demonstrate both sound judgement and initiative, both qualities which will prepare them for effective leadership within schools.

The PGCE M-level means that you will develop the knowledge and understanding of educational theory and the skills and attributes which enable you not only to apply your thinking to your own professional practice but also will prepare you to lead the practice of others in the future. Therefore the PGCE M-level is an enhanced model to that provided by the PGCE H-level.

However, let us just remember one important point. The PGCE is not a Masters award and the statements for the FHEQ were written as 'exit' statements, that is for someone who has been awarded a Masters. This means that, just like your honours award, you will be developing the knowledge, skills and attributes outlined in the framework throughout your work at Masters level, including the PGCE at M-level.

Finally, let us explore the idea that doing a PGCE M-level adds little to the skills required for effective practice in the classroom. It is true that the PGCE H-level was designed to meet the professional requirements for a beginning teacher and has succeeded in producing very good teachers for a great many years. You might think, therefore, that there is no need to change something which has worked so well for so long. However, with the rate of change in education and the enhanced professional requirements for moving up the career ladder, many have felt that a shift is required from teacher *training* to teacher *education*. This shift requires that teachers are able to think critically about education and the way in which it can best be interpreted, not only for the next five years but for the whole of a teacher's career. There is a saying in education that the only thing constant is change and this is certainly true, with not a year going by without some new initiative, directive or regulation. The changes proposed by the Coalition at the time of writing are no exception: these changes will impact on all aspects of education from the nature and delivery mode of the curriculum to the management and structure of schools themselves. The introduction of the English Baccalaureate, linking success at secondary level to the coverage of specific academic subjects (awarded to any student who gains five good GCSE or iGCSE passes in English, Mathematics, the Sciences, a modern or ancient foreign language and a humanities subject) emphasizes a significant move away from the vocational agenda introduced during the previous government term. Perhaps the biggest educational intention of the current government is that ultimately all state schools will be academies or Free Schools; instead of a state education system the proposal is a network of privately sponsored and independently managed state-funded individual schools. A system of this type may well impact on teacher pay, conditions of employment and transferability within the network, as the academies and Free Schools will not have to follow the National Curriculum. Running parallel with this are the proposed changes to teacher training and practice: the school improvement policy underpinning these changes is based on raising the quality of teaching and teachers. The role of universities in teacher training will also change with the introduction and development of 'teaching schools'. The proposals to transform teacher training aligns with the 'Teach First' training model: a model which trains graduates with appropriate qualifications (a 2.2 degree or above) for six weeks, then places them in school. The assumption is that the student teacher will remain in school for a few years before moving into leadership.

Whatever changes are bestowed on the profession, the recognized need to continue to develop the professionalism of teachers means that there is now a real opportunity to take teacher education to the next level, a notion at the heart of which lies the idea of the 'visionary teacher': the teacher who can respond to the multitude of changes which will occur throughout their career by drawing on theory and research and by possessing the skills of critical evaluation and reflection which will enable them to make changes in their practice which account for this.

At the heart of the development of the PGCE M-level, as Figure 1.2 shows, is the philosophy that the developing professional requires an understanding of research, theory and practice in order to be effective throughout their career.

Examples of how this can be put into effect can be found in later chapters; however, it could be argued that this relationship is also integral to the PGCE H-level, so just how different are the two? Let us start by exploring the idea of 'professional teacher'. Figure 1.2 shows that in order to develop as a professional there is an integral relationship between theory, research and practice. It is this which will enable teachers to continue to develop their own practice throughout their career. It is this which enables the professional to both anticipate and respond to the almost constant changes in education.

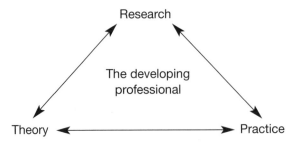

Figure 1.2 Model of the developing professional

The perceived role of a professional teacher has changed significantly over the years, alongside educational policy, initiatives, strategies and directives. If you were to interview a teacher from the 1970s or early 1980s their view of professionalism may be very different from that of a teacher nowadays. It is likely that their emphasis would have been on the full creative process of reviewing, designing and evaluating curriculum guidelines: developing and planning their own curriculum in the light of advances and developments within their own subject area and education generally. The curriculum was not static, and lively and fruitful dialogues were established between teachers from neighbouring schools as well as between universities and schools. Continuing professional development activities focused on updating subject knowledge and understanding, techniques and procedures, as well as developing pedagogy. Experienced teachers of today may recognize some similarities with current practice, but the focus is very different.

Perhaps the most important factor in changes to the professionalism of teachers has been the implementation of centrally prescribed curriculum guidelines which began in the mid-1980s. These guidelines, which included the National Curriculum, GCSE and AS/A2 criteria and syllabuses, were produced to provide a framework for subject teachers to operate in. The quality of education, and indeed the pupils' attainment, was largely down to the way these guidelines were interpreted and implemented (Rawling, 2003), and following the introduction of the National Curriculum in 1989 Roberts (1995) noted that one of the biggest changes this introduction brought about was how teachers perceived their role. She explained that the new curriculum seemed to negate teacher involvement and refocused curriculum control at a national level. The impact of this tended to find teachers 'delivering' the curriculum rather than interpreting or engaging with it. The curriculum presented one set of approved knowledge and skills, of which the content appeared static, and this, in itself, limited the need for updating and creative thought. Liaison with universities and the productive dialogues of the past became increasingly inappropriate as autonomy on the part of the teacher seemed to wane. Owing to increasing administrative pressures, cooperative work with other schools also declined and in-service opportunities assumed a different focus, relating more to delivery and assessment and management issues than being 'subject' related. At the same time, teacher education changed and the restructured courses included limited subject-based training. This meant that newly qualified teachers, especially at primary level, were struggling to interpret the curriculum for those areas that were outside of their specialism. At secondary level, specialism content was sometimes far removed from the subject studied at undergraduate level.

Since the late 1990s and into the early 2000s there has been an increasing drive from central government to shift curriculum planning back to the subject teacher.

A significant move away from the prescriptive nature of the now defunct Qualifications and Curriculum Authority's (QCA) Schemes of Work to more personalized schemes and creativity gained status within the educational community towards the end of 2010. The changes to the curriculum implemented through the Primary Strategy and the Secondary National Strategy (2008 onwards) afforded the potential to resurrect levels of autonomy within the profession, despite the continued 'accountability' approach to assessment that continued to straitjacket progress (Ross et al., 2010). For some, however, especially those within the Coalition government, this increased level of autonomy was a move too far. At the time of writing the revised National Curriculum has been through the early stages of consultation. The new curriculum aims to raise standards by providing opportunities for all children to acquire a core of essential knowledge in the key subjects and beyond that for teachers to have the freedom to use their professionalism and expertise to help all children realize their potential.

Although the approaches suggested by the Coalition government have caused considerable consternation among the education fraternity, this increased emphasis on professionalism and teacher autonomy, at least beyond the core subjects, is important as it enables those of us who have continued to recognize the value of such qualities as creativity and autonomy in curriculum and lesson design and see this as a driving force within the profession to use the prescribed guidelines as initially intended, *as guidelines*: a platform from which to enthuse and inspire pupils. The PGCE M-level is built on this understanding, requiring trainees not simply to accept prescription but rather to analyse its effectiveness and adapt it to suit the individuals in their class or their school.

Research undertaken by Rawling (2003) into developing professionalism among geography teachers identified five aspects of professionalism (see Table 1.1):

- interacting with pupils;

- interacting with other teachers;

- valuing him or herself professionally;

- interacting with the wider subject community;

- interacting with state and policy-making.

Table 1.1 Being professional as a teacher (Rawling, 2003)

	Continuum of characteristics of professionalism	
Aspects of professionalism	**Fully developed professionalism**	**Restricted professionalism**
How the teacher interacts with pupils	Focusing on the needs of individuals and how to develop each to own potential. Focusing on variety of teaching and learning strategies to fit each situation.	Focusing on the needs of the group to bring as many as possible to the required level/ standard. Focusing on transmission/ direct teaching to ensure required detailed content is 'delivered'.
How the teacher interacts with other teachers	Working in cooperation, emphasis on teamwork at school and subject level. Professional development activities focus on new ideas, creativity and reflecting on own classrooms.	Working as an individual teacher and/or subject department in competition with those in other schools. Professional development focuses on 'tips for teaching' and how to manage and 'deliver' national curriculum/assessment requirements.

How the teacher values him/ herself professionally	Gaining enjoyment and satisfaction from finding out about new developments in education, research and in society.	Finding no relevance in and/ or time to follow up new developments in the wider educational context.
	Seeing out-of-school hobbies and interests as feeding into personal development and professional creativity.	Seeing school and 'outside school' as separate existences with no beneficial overlap or creative interchange.
How the teacher interacts with the wider subject community	Participating in interchange and updating activities with subject colleagues at all levels from higher education to primary education.	Seeing the subject in school and in higher education as being separate systems and therefore no need for interchange.
	Having an interest in the subject, its character and relevance to society.	Accepting the national requirements as the definition of the subject and seeing no need for debate.
How the teacher interacts with the state and policy-making	Making a valued contribution to discussions about the appropriate national frameworks for the subject (need to be creative).	Seen as the 'technician' trained to deliver knowledge, understanding, skills prescribed by the state (need to be competent).
	Seen as a creative professional who is trusted to make decisions about subject and classroom matters.	Not envisaged as needing to make important decisions about subject or pedagogy and generally not trusted to do so.

 Activity

Thinking about the areas identified in Table 1.1, how would you distinguish between being a 'reflective' and a 'reflexive' professional? Some ideas are given later in the chapter.

Perhaps the most important quality identified in Table 1.1 relates to how you value your own development as a teacher. Achieving QTS is only the very first step on your career journey, a journey that needs constant reviewing, revisiting and evaluating. During that time you will need to keep abreast of developments within your specialist subject, education generally and related research and use these to impact on your practice. Education, as mentioned above, is not static but is an evolving entity that demands an input of energy to keep it fresh and dynamic. During the PGCE M-level programme you will be encouraged to develop your reflective, reflexive and critically analytical skills, setting you well on the path of the 'visionary teacher'.

Let us consider your developing understanding of teaching, learning and behaviour management as a beginning teacher. As you start your training you will probably find that much of your focus is on your role as the teacher and the ways in which you can get children to behave sufficiently for you to get to the end of the lesson (no mean feat with some classes!). As you become more skilled in behaviour management you will then be able to turn your attention to the learning taking place in your classroom and analysis of your own teaching will become more critically evaluative. You will consider what you did well and why this led to new learning and you will be all too aware of what did not go well, although you may not always understand why or how to move forward. As you move into the first year of teaching you will continue to develop, extending your range of teaching approaches, developing a greater range of behaviour management strategies and honing your skills in differentiating learning so that it moves from whole-class to more individualized and personalized approaches. This process will be a constant element of your developing career in teaching. The curriculum will change, teaching approaches will evolve and, most importantly, each child will respond differently to the approaches you adopt (sometimes on a daily basis), requiring you to continually review and develop your own skills and understanding in these areas. The key to this development is criticality, the ability to review approaches in a way which draws on current research and theory about how children learn and use this to determine how you will personalize learning in a way which provides the opportunity for all learners to achieve their full potential.

Although the PGCE M-level may provide you with a critical understanding of only a small part of that expected later in your career, you will already have developed the skills which enable you to think at this level and therefore will be able to transfer these skills into other aspects of your work within the classroom. You will know where to go to support your developing thinking and how to analyse critically and evaluate current theory and research in this area. You will have developed skills in independent and autonomous study and be able to apply your thinking creatively and with some originality. In other words, you will already be well on the road to thinking in the ways expected from teachers much further up the career ladder.

 Activity outcome: Reflexive vs reflective

Look back at your responses to the earlier activity and consider again the idea of reflexivity and reflectivity.

Being reflexive is a specific example of being reflective. When you reflect on something you look back at it and analyse what went on, deciding, for example, what was good and what needs improvement. When you are being reflexive you take into account the impact and implications that you as a teacher will bring to, and have on, a particular learning situation. For example, you have your own bias, values and indeed your own 'persona' that could influence how you teach and what and how the pupils learn. You need to be aware of this and not prejudice the learning situation by your own direct influence.

Reflective Activity

Spend some time in a school identifying the aspects of a fully developed professional. Observe an experienced teacher and, using Table 1.1 as your reference, identify what it is that they do in practice. For example, how do they interact with pupils? How do they focus on the needs of individuals? What teaching and learning strategies do they use to enable each pupil to make progress?

If possible, talk through your observations with the teacher at some point following your observation to see if there are other things they are doing which you have either not observed or have not been aware of them doing. Remember that good teaching is often very subtle in its approach. It is often difficult to identify what an experienced teacher seems to do with ease.

Now draw up a list which identifies the types of practice you would wish to use in your own classroom. What have you learned about effective teaching and learning and how might you convey this?

This is a particularly useful activity to do prior to attending an interview for a place on a teacher training course as it will prepare you for the types of questions you may be asked and demonstrate that not only have you visited schools but that you are capable of reflecting on and learning from your experience.

Education in Scotland

The Scottish Parliament (1999) in their Subject Map on Education described the Scottish education system as being '. . . quite distinct from the education systems of the United Kingdom' (p. 1). This distinction arises from several factors.

The Scottish system has its own legislative framework

As in England, the Scottish legal framework is based on a series of Scottish Education Acts. The entire education system from pre-school to higher education and life-long learning is the responsibility of the Scottish Parliament. The Scottish Executive is responsible for policy development; the Scottish Office Education Department administers national education policy and the Scottish local authorities oversee provision in their local schools and pre-schools.

Curriculum framework

In 2004 the 'Curriculum for Excellence' was introduced replacing the existing non-statutory curriculum guidelines. This 3–18 curriculum aims to ensure all children and young people in Scotland develop the perceived attributes, knowledge and skills they need to flourish in life, learning and work. These skills and attributes relate to four capacities which the curriculum seeks to develop:

- Successful learners

- Confident individuals

- Responsible citizens

- Effective contributors

The curriculum aims to provide each child and young person with the relevant set of experiences to develop these skills and attributes directly through the curriculum subjects: interdisciplinary learning, school ethos and specific opportunities for personal achievement, building on the contributions afforded by the wider informal education experiences. These experiences and outcomes signpost progression in learning and form the cornerstones of student development and targeting setting.

Table 1.2 shows the progression of qualifications in the Scottish education system while Table 1.3 shows the way in which the Scottish system equates to that in England.

Table 1.2 Qualification progression in the Scottish system

S3 and S4	S5	S6
Standard Grade (Foundation Level) / Access 3	Intermediate 1	Intermediate 2
Standard Grade (General Level) or Intermediate 1	Intermediate 2	Higher
Standard Grade (Credit Level) or Intermediate 2	Higher	Advanced Higher

Table 1.3 The Scottish education system and English equivalents

Year	Age range	England equivalent
Primary (P) 1	4–6	Year 1
P2	5–7	Year 2
P3	6–8	Year 3
P4	7–9	Year 4
P5	8–10	Year 5
P6	9–11	Year 6
P7	10–12	Year 7
Secondary (S) 1	11–13	Year 8
S2	12–14	Year 9
S3	13–15	Year 10
S4	14–16	Year 11
S5	15–17	Year 12
S6	16–18	Year 13

Qualifying to teach in Scotland

While the philosophical principles underpinning everything written above apply equally to the all the devolved nations, the detail of the education system, the curriculum and the training process varies significantly in Scotland and warrants a specific mention.

There are several ways to qualify as a teacher in Scotland, depending initially on your target age group and the nature of the course you wish to take (see Table 1.4).

Table 1.4 Qualifying as a teacher in Scotland

Primary – 2 main routes	Secondary – 3 main routes
The four-year Bachelor of Education (BEd) degree	The four year Bachelor of Education (BEd) degree or a combined degree course at a Scottish university
The one-year full-time Professional Graduate Diploma in Education (PGDE)	The one-year, full-time Professional Graduate Diploma in Education (PGDE)
	PGDE courses, that are part-time and/or distance learning
	For secondary teaching in Scotland, your degree must be relevant to the subject you wish to teach

Successfully qualifying at a Scottish university entitles you to teach in a Scottish school. Allocation of students for school experience is managed and organized by a local authority and quality assured by the National Strategy Group covering student placements. Representatives from interested parties across the education sector sit on this group whose main aim is to maintain a strategic overview of student placements in Scotland, to work closely with all the relevant stakeholders and to ensure consistency of national practice.

Once qualified, all Scottish trained teachers are guaranteed a one-year teaching post in a Scottish local authority under the national induction programme for newly qualified teachers. Teachers are allocated to one of five local authorities of their choosing. The Teacher Induction Scheme has gained international recognition. Teachers on the programme have a maximum class commitment time equal to 70 per cent that of a full-time teacher, with the rest of the time devoted to their professional development. All have access to the services of an experienced teacher as a mentor. By the end of their one-year induction, they should be ready to gain full registration with the General Teaching Council for Scotland.

A national framework for continuing professional development (CPD) is in place to enable teachers at every stage in their career to realize their potential and to develop and maintain skills. The Scottish government funds a national database of CPD supported by the National CPD Team and Learning and Teaching Scotland. An annual Scottish Learning Festival organized by Learning and Teaching Scotland and held every September in Glasgow is the largest national educational conference and exhibition in Scotland.

Chartered teacher status was introduced as a means of rewarding teachers who want to further their career but stay in the classroom. There are chartered teachers in each local authority and more and more teachers are signing up for the programme.

Summary

It should now be clear to you that there are differences between studying the PGCE at M-level and at H-level and that the decision of which route to take is very much a personal choice, based on the level of challenge you want in both your training and your future career. While it is true that the PGCE M-level does present greater academic challenge, this is something that you have already demonstrated that you can respond to successfully and there is no reason to assume that you would not be able to do so again. The move from level 6 to level 7 presents no greater challenge than moving from level 4 to level 5 or from level 5 to level 6. In terms of workload, the PGCE M-level is no more demanding than the PGCE H-level and may even be less. Also, there is likely to be more autonomy in the PGCE M-level than in the PGCE H-level, as independent, autonomous working is a requirement of M-level study. The enhancement offered by the PGCE M-level to developing professionalism in terms of education as a whole and to you personally is evident and should not be easily dismissed. We have heard trainees bemoan the fact that they 'just want to be a teacher'; our response is that there is no such thing as 'just a teacher'. The following chapters provide more details about the ways in which the PGCE M-level enhances the profession, but if you are still trying to make up your mind as to which route to follow, you may find the following questions useful.

- What award do I want to gain (Postgraduate or Professional Certificate in Education, or perhaps another route into teaching) and how does this support my personal and professional aspirations?

- Do I have the appropriate degree classification for the award and institution of my choice?

- How many assignments do I want to do and at what level? (This is particularly important when the institution requires you to do assessments at both level 7 and level 6, which may be the equivalent of 120 credit points.)

- What kind of assessment do I feel most comfortable with (e.g. theoretical written essays, presentations, small-scale research)?

- Is the course I am considering organized in such a way as to enable me to develop my own independence and autonomy?

- With which school placement arrangement do I feel most comfortable? Look carefully at the number of placements and the amount of time you spend in each school.

- What opportunities can the institution offer me to meet some of the specific needs I have in terms of where I will be seeking employment? For example, if you wish to work in an inner-city school, will you have access to these types of experiences during the period of your training?

- What support will the institution offer for preparing to work at M-level, and is it appropriate to my needs?

- If I choose to articulate my M-level credit points from the PGCE into a Masters award, will the institution of my choice accept the modules I will take with me and the number of credit points? (This is particularly important if you will complete more than 60 credit points at M-level as some institutions will only allow articulation of this amount into an existing Masters award – see Chapter 7 for further details on this.)

- Do I have the time and the commitment to pursue a challenging course of study at this time?

Although some of these questions are very personal to you, the information you require to answer them can usually be found in the prospectus for an institution. The website relating to the course is a good starting place and the programme specification will provide much of the information you require.

Further reading

www.ltscotland.org.uk – Learning and Teaching Scotland is a useful portal for reference to the Scottish education system

www.qaa.ac.uk – the Quality Assurance Agency is the central government site for higher education and the quality assurance mechanisms which underpin it.

http://www.qaa.ac.uk/Publications/InformationAndGuidance/Documents/FHEQ08.pdf – this site gives the framework for higher education qualifications in England, Wales and Northern Ireland.

www.scotland.gov.uk – the Scottish government portal which provides access to the education and training pages.

www.tda.gov.uk – the website for the Training and Development Agency for Schools which provides key information for anyone wishing to enter teacher training.

www.tda.gov.uk/teachers/professionalstandards.aspx – provides access to the Professional Standards for Teachers and trainee teachers.

References

Lakin, L. (2004) 'The golden age of protein: an initial teacher training perspective on the biological role of proteins in our everyday lives', *International Journal of Consumer Studies*, 28 (2): 127–34.

QAA (Quality Assurance Agency) (2001) *The Framework for Higher Education Qualifications in England, Wales and Northern Ireland*. London: QAA.

Rawling, E. (2003) *Connecting Policy and Practice: Research in Geography Education*. Nottingham: BERA.

Roberts, M. (1995) 'Interpretation of the Geography National Curriculum: a common curriculum for all?', *Journal of Curriculum Studies*, 27 (2): 187–205.

Ross, K., Lakin, L. and McKechnie, J. (2010) *Teaching Secondary Science*. Abingdon: Routledge.

Scottish Parliament (1999) *Education in Scotland, Devolved Areas Series/10*, 16 June.

TDA (Training and Development Agency for Schools) (2007) *Professional Standards for Teachers*. London: TDA.

2

What can I expect my PGCE at M-level to look like at subject level?

Liz Lakin

In this chapter we focus on your development as a competent teacher within the subject areas you will be teaching. It aims to:

- explore the idea of you as a learner and as an educator;

- enable you to understand the place of the subject within the PGCE M-level programme;

- support you in taking ownership of the development of your own subject knowledge and understanding;

- help you to identify the ways in which theory and research can enable you to support pupils' development of subject knowledge and understanding;

- explore the relationship between learning and teaching and enable you to reflect on the range of approaches to both.

Many of the examples used are drawn from science education, but you will find that they fit well with all subjects across the curriculum.

The subject specialist and competent teacher

In keeping with the Professional Standards for Qualified Teacher Status, a primary PGCE M-level course aims to prepare you to plan, teach and assess the subjects of the National

Curriculum effectively with particular emphasis on the core subjects (English, mathematics, science) and information and communication technology (ICT), while a secondary course aims to facilitate transition from a subject expert to competent teacher, who is confident in teaching all aspects of their chosen subject at the appropriate level. Both courses also aim to enable you to develop a range of skills and abilities that will contribute to your effectiveness as a professional educator and reflective practitioner. For you to achieve this, not only do you need to feel confident and competent as a teacher, you need to be comfortable with your subject knowledge and understanding.

An introduction to the curriculum and its supporting literature

Early on in any PGCE course you will be introduced to the wealth of statutory and non-statutory material supporting the education curriculum of your chosen age range. This may include documentation for the Foundation Stage, the Primary and Secondary strategies, departmental schemes of work and examination specifications. It will also include the National Curriculum: the legal requirements for the curriculum together with supporting information to help teachers implement these requirements in school (DfEE and QCA, 1999). The structure, emphasis and assessment procedure may differ depending upon what part of the UK you teach in, but the specific content is largely the same. Activities such as the following example of a university-based session will be available during your college or university programme to help you find your way through the relevant documentation.

 Decoding the science curriculum

This session is designed to give students a beginner's awareness of the statutory frameworks that support secondary science education and to update current practice compared with their own experience as school-age pupils. Typically this involves looking at the present and the proposed Key Stage 3 framework, discussion of the different routes through GCSE and identification of a typical route that runs from the National Curriculum through QCA and departmental schemes of work, where the national strategy for science fits and how this whole framework supports a teacher planning a lesson, or more accurately a sequence of lessons. One of the activities the students engage with is to map an idea or concept across the curriculum, including looking at the range of routes through GCSE. The activity helps the students to fit the different pieces of documentation together while preparing them for their initial visits to school and their future subject-based assignment.

Although this example was drawn from science education, similar sessions will take place in other specialisms at secondary and across the core and foundation subjects at primary.

Reflective Activity

Subject teaching changes significantly over time and it is important for you to not only keep pace with these changes but begin to predict what changes may happen so that you can be more proactive in your response. For example, as little as 25 years ago secondary science teaching focused on a process-led approach giving rise to curricula which were led primarily by developing the skills and processes of investigation and enquiry. Today, largely as a result of a clearer understanding of how children learn, the emphasis is much more on a balance between conceptual and procedural development. There are advantages and disadvantages with each approach, however, and it is left to teachers to determine how best to deliver the curriculum in a way which enables all learners to achieve their potential.

Read professional literature, such as the *Times Educational Supplement* and websites and magazines relating to your chosen subject area. From this reading identify what you feel are the main issues, challenges or opportunities. Now identify how the current curriculum and teaching and learning approaches reflect these and promote learning. Are there any conflicts between the statutory curriculum, theories of learning and the needs of learners? Are there areas which are underdeveloped? Can you predict how your subject area may develop over the next ten years? How might you respond to these changes in your classroom?

Developing your subject knowledge

On a primary course, subject knowledge and understanding of the three core subjects will be developed via taught sessions at university or college. The core skills of ICT need to be integrated across all curriculum areas and it is therefore considered a vital part of the core curriculum. This will usually be taught alongside these subject areas. Religious education, PSHE or citizenship and the foundation subjects (art and design, design and technology, humanities (history and geography), music and physical education) are introduced to varying degrees on different courses, ranging from taster days to more in-depth studies. Some courses also offer additional specialisms, such as French, although it is now a requirement that all primary trainees are introduced to the teaching of a modern foreign language (MFL). It would be worth exploring which course offers expertise in the area you are particularly interested in.

At secondary level the emphasis is on your own subject specialism. Most student teachers would have specialized in one aspect of the school curriculum and usually have specialized further within that subject; for example, a science student teacher could be a qualified nuclear physicist, a biochemist or an archaeologist. All will be training to teach science at secondary school level. They will probably need, however, to develop their subject knowledge in at least one if not two of the three sciences. For this reason subject knowledge support sessions are available, usually before, but sometimes during, the university or college course. This applies equally to other specialisms; for example, mathematicians may come from an accountancy background and future art teachers may have a background in fine art and design and will need to 'brush up' on other areas of the art curriculum.

Taking ownership of your subject knowledge and understanding (SKU)

It is worth remembering that throughout life we go on learning, hence the term 'life-long learning', and this can take place in any aspect of our life – your subject knowledge and understanding is no exception. You will not only discover gaps in your subject knowledge but also some misbeliefs or misconceptions. You may have carried these with you from your own schooling or merely acquired them as you grew up. For example, when asked why the sky is blue, several students answer 'Oh, I always thought it was blue because it reflects the sea.' It is only those students who are familiar with refraction who can explain that white light is scattered by particles in the atmosphere; blue light is scattered the most, so we see the sky as blue.

So, how will you know about these gaps in your knowledge and these misconceptions that you may hold? First consider the learning process as going on a journey: you know where you want to get to, or at least you have an idea, you know the 'mode of transport' you will use, be it books, the Internet, your peers and so on. You may even have mapped out a route to take you there, but do you know where you are starting from? This is crucial to any journey, but sometimes we may think we are at the 'start' because it meets all the relevant criteria. You can even talk yourself into believing it is correct, whereas you are in fact starting from somewhere totally different, as explained in this case study.

In search of Aira Force *or* How not to climb Helvellyn

The postcard 'easy walks' guide outlined an interesting walk starting and finishing at a car park and taking in the sights of the magnificent Aira Force waterfall in the Lake District. It would take an hour and landmarks were set out to guide the way. What could be easier? The problem is, one car park looks very much like another along this stretch of road, even down to the river running alongside and the information building – which was closed. So you decide that you are at the right place and maybe that wooden bridge over the river could be interpreted as a stile. Not having explored the area before, you walk on, enjoying the view, not too worried that the stated 'spectacular views of the lake' in reality seem to be masked by a row of tall full-foliaged trees. An hour passes with no waterfall in sight. You walk on, just over the next rise and around that hill, making a few excuses for the passing landmarks. The walk stretches for miles, and it climbs. You do likewise; well, you've come this far! A fellow traveller comes striding by and you engage in conversation, mentioning Aira Force and your seeming inadequacies in 'postcard' map-reading. To your dismay you discover that the car park for the much sought after waterfall is a couple of miles further up the road; apparently you really can't miss it. To make matters worse, you are now two hours along the upward track to Helvellyn, one of the highest fells in the Lake District, and not best prepared. (See note at the end of the chapter.)

So how does this tale relate to learning and subject knowledge? Too often as teachers we make assumptions. For example, according to the spiralling National Curriculum, pupils in Key Stage 1 learn counting up to 20 and by Key Stage 2 should be proficient at this; therefore teachers do not need to cover it again. We know, however, from experience that this may not be the case and the astute teacher will revisit this before progressing. Likewise, you as a learner will need to check that your starting point is where you think it is. It is common in science education to set a series of 'elicitation exercises' at the beginning of a new topic to establish this baseline. For example, when introducing 'thermal insulation' a useful question to pose might be:

If you wrap a block of ice cream in a blanket, will it melt (a) faster; (b) slower; or (c) at the same rate as one left in the room unwrapped?

What is this question trying to find out? Think about each of the alternative answers and work through the 'thought pathways' that someone giving that answer may be taking. Why, for instance, would someone think the wrapped block of ice cream would melt faster? Presumably because they think the wrapping is making it warmer. Where might they get that idea? In reality the ice cream will melt slower because the wrapping acts a barrier, or insulator, between the coldness of the ice cream and the relative warmth of the surrounding air.

Questions like these help the teacher and they should help you, as a learner, to assess these 'thought pathways', enabling you to identify areas of unfamiliarity as well as areas of misconception. Your PGCE M-level course will introduce a range of strategies to help you assess your own subject knowledge baseline. Often a subject knowledge audit is used based on the key concept areas and ideas. The outcomes of this audit will inform your self-study requirements and ensure you reach the necessary level of subject knowledge and understanding as identified in the Professional Standards for QTS.

As a professional teacher you will need to go beyond just being up to speed with your subject knowledge. You need to be thinking carefully about how this knowledge works, not just within its own field but also in relation to other areas of the curriculum. For example, how are the key concepts of the core subjects and ICT integrated and what are the problems arising when they do? ICT is a case in point. You can plan a lesson in English incorporating ICT, but is the learning 'literacy based' or is it masked by the use of the technology? This is an easy trap to fall into and one that needs careful consideration.

Not only do you need to think laterally about the subject, you need to consider how the various concepts within the subject progress. Meyer and Land (2003) describe conceptual progression in terms of threshold concepts. These are ideas that, once understood, pave the way for further development and understanding within the subject. If these are not understood, however, the learner may be prohibited from progressing further. From an economics perspective, one such concept would be 'opportunity costs'. Consider the following elicitation question:

> When you have to make a difficult decision or choice do you: think that there is no choice at all and the outcome is already predetermined; consider all the alternatives and their immediate consequences; or consider all the alternatives and recognize that there are two sides to each one, each with its own associated cost? (After Meyer and Land, 2003)

Think carefully about what this question is exploring and explain why the ideas could be termed 'threshold concepts' (some suggestions are presented on page 36).

Another example, this time from the science curriculum, specifically 'plate tectonics', might be the following:

> Could the dinosaurs have walked from Europe to America?

Once again, think carefully about what this question is exploring and explain why the ideas could be termed 'threshold concepts'.

Having gained an insight into how the PGCE M-level can help you take ownership for the development of your subject knowledge, we now turn to how this is applied in the teaching environment.

The professional educator

A qualified teacher is expected to draw on a range of teaching, learning and behaviour management strategies, knowing how to use them effectively and adapt them if necessary. This should include personalized learning, thereby allowing all pupils to achieve their potential. To address these requirements PGCE M-level courses aim to equip you with a rigorous knowledge and understanding of the core areas of education: teaching, learning and assessment, professional values and practice. This can be translated into the pedagogic approaches, theories and research underpinning effective teaching within the various subject areas. So what does all this mean and how does it translate into practice in the classroom?

'Pedagogy' is a difficult word to define. In most contexts it is the term given to the ways in which the complex relationships between views of knowledge and ideas about learning, teaching, learning about learning (meta-learning) and the learning environment in its broadest sense (physical, social and political) are integrated and managed within the classroom. This integration and management is subject to a range of external influencing factors. To help on this pathway, let's consider what we understand by the term 'knowledge' and becoming 'knowledgeable'.

 Activity

So far we have considered how you can develop your SKU, but what does the term 'knowledge' actually mean to you? Bruner (1996) warns that knowledge is too often construed as a product rather than a process and often pupils and indeed some teachers see the process of becoming more knowledgeable as topping up or soaking up information and facts.

How do you perceive 'knowledge'? Is it something that can be acquired or 'topped up', like adding to your collection of model cars, handbags or shoes, most of which will stay in the cupboard or on the shelf and never be used? Or do you see it as an input of information that needs assimilating and reformulating so it becomes owned by you, to be used at a later, relevant date?

 Activity

Now consider where this knowledge acquisition may take place – the 'learning environment' – and who the key players are, for example the learner, their peers, you the teacher and possibly the teaching assistant. What do you think are the main external influences affecting the integration and management of all those factors mentioned in the definition of pedagogy above? Some suggestions are given in Table 2.3 on page 37.

The learning process: theories

Having explored our understanding of knowledge and the influencing factors affecting learners in the learning environment, we now turn our attention to the learning process itself.

 Activity

What is learning, and how does it take place? Consider for a moment what you understand by the verb 'to learn'. How do you know when you have learnt something and how has that learning taken place?

Kyriacou suggests that 'Pupil learning can be defined as changes in a pupil's behaviours which takes place as a result of being engaged in an educational experience' (1998: 22). This therefore suggests the capacity to do something different from what could be done earlier (Schunk, 1996). How does this stand with your own interpretation of learning?

Each student brings his or her own level of expertise and specialist knowledge to their PGCE M-level course. This means that within any one cohort of students the level and range of subject knowledge may be vast. Likewise, pupils will bring to your lessons their unique experiences, knowledge and understanding, including areas of strength and weaknesses. As a teacher you need to be able to tap into these areas, developing the strengths and addressing the weaknesses. With a class of 30 or so pupils this is not easy. An understanding of the way pupils learn, how they assimilate ideas and how these ideas become permanent is an important measure in assisting with this process. 'Teaching and learning' underpins all PGCE courses by integrating important facets of educational theory, such as learning theory and teaching styles, with subject knowledge and practical application.

There are many theories and approaches to teaching and learning, and you will need to be familiar with the most popular as well as aware of current developments. These are explored further in this chapter and in Chapter 4. The PGCE M-level course provides opportunities for you to explore and discuss contemporary and more established ideas within this field, through the taught educational studies session and also through the subject-based assignments. Often, at least one of the M-level assignments will be pedagogy related, asking you to evaluate critically current theories of learning which underpin approaches within either your specific subject area (secondary) or a chosen subject area (primary). You may be asked to examine this in the light of curriculum change and development, evaluating how these theories are applied in practice and commenting on possible areas for improvement. Examples of a possible focus might include:

- classroom displays and constructivism in literacy lessons;

- social constructivism and talk in primary science;

- model-based teaching in secondary geography.

But where do you start? The activities below introduce you to the more popular ideas within teaching and learning and then explain how they may be applied at the subject level.

 Activity

Research has identified many ideas about learning and these have been built up into theories and recognized approaches to teaching and learning. First, what do you understand as the difference between a theory and an approach?

Table 2.1 lists some recognized theories and approaches to teaching and learning. Their definitions have been mixed up; match the theory or approach to its appropriate definition.

Table 2.1 Theories and approaches to teaching

Theories and approaches	Definition
Co-constructed learning	(1) In the form popularized (though not invented) by Alistair Smith, this approach draws heavily on brain-based learning. Building on neuro-linguistic programming it offers strategies that would enable students to learn more naturally, more effectively and faster. Smith's approach advocates a four-stage learning cycle: connect, activate, demonstrate, consolidate.
Accelerated learning	(2) Systematic development of the skills, dispositions and knowledge needed to become an effective, independent learner. An important component of this approach is students reflecting on, learning about and learning for the learning process itself.
Differentiated learning	(3) A new term for an old idea. Learning is most effective when it is designed jointly by the teacher and students through a process of negotiation.
Constructivism	(4) Based on the work of Black and Wiliam from King's College London, this approach now features in the national strategies. Their research demonstrated that giving students regular, diagnostic, precise, actionable, written or verbal feedback is probably the most powerful way to improve performance.

Learning to learn and meta-learning	(5) A current government drive, that has become a buzzword, officially defined as 'tailoring education to individual needs, interests and aptitudes so as to ensure that every pupil achieves and reaches the highest standards possible' (DfES Standards).
Thinking skills and metacognition	(6) A relatively old philosophical position that learning cannot be transferred. It can only be constructed in the mind of each learner, who must make their own meaning based on what they bring to the learning experience (in terms of prior knowledge, understanding, misunderstanding, baggage and so on). This fundamental notion has been confirmed by the findings of neuroscience and has been given new life: learning is a mentally active process.
Assessment for learning	(7) Deliberate development of students' thinking capacities. Various models and programmes exist, such as CASE and Philosophy for Children. The McGuinness Report (1999) effectively determined five cross-phase and cross-curricular categories associated with this, together with the process of reflecting on and gaining control over one's own thinking behaviours.
Personalized learning	(8) The long-standing idea that learning activities, resources and support should be matched as precisely as possible to learners' individual needs, be they 'gifted and talented' or 'challenged' in some way. The intention is that every single student should receive the most appropriate curriculum and learning experience.

The answers are provided in Table 2.4 on page 37. One approach not included in the table is 'active learning'. What do you understand by this term and why do you think it has not been included?

The learning process: application

Now we look at how these theories and approaches can be applied at the subject level. During your time in school and at the taught sessions in university or college you will be encouraged to consider their application. Modelling of good practice is a key aim of the PGCE M-level course and you will come across several examples. The following is taken from a subject knowledge session on human blood circulation.

During this session the approach used was one of reflection and debate; students were encouraged to consider the 'big picture' view of the topic in question. For example, a graph of the cardiac cycle together with an ECG readout and phonocardiogram were discussed. The link between the electrical stimulus, characteristic sound of the heartbeat, the sequence of heart muscle contraction and the circulating blood were all taken into account. This was a move away from the more isolated, reductionist approach that is too often afforded to the teaching of biology (Ross et al., 2004). Being used to a 'regurgitation style' assessment process, the students initially found it difficult to see beyond the detail. Throughout the module they were encouraged to reflect upon their own learning. A confidence quiz helped with this. The students were given a list of subject-related statements and asked to identify whether or not they were correct. They were then asked to qualify their answer on a five-point confidence scale. This served to highlight areas for development but also identified students who felt confident about a particular statement that was in fact incorrect, something that was surprisingly common.

 Activity

Identify at least three different learning approaches used in the case study described above.

In an effective learning environment, you will see not only a range of teaching and learning approaches used but also a range of learning styles being accommodated for. Watkins (2006) suggests that the term 'learning styles' encompasses the established idea that people naturally learn in different ways. Over the years many attempts have been made to create models, probably the most widespread and well-known being VAK (visual, auditory and kinaesthetic).

 Activity

Some of these styles and models have been identified in Table 2.2. Once again, their definitions have been mixed up. Match the style, construct or model to its appropriate definition. The answers are provided in Table 2.5 on page 38.

Table 2.2 Learning styles, construct and models

Learnable intelligence	(1) Emphasizes the biological and unavoidable dominance of emotions in all human behaviour. For learning to succeed teachers and students need to be familiar with these influences.
Emotional intelligence	(2) The idea that intelligence cannot be easily measured or used to make comparative judgements because it is not a single quality. The most popular proponent is Professor Howard Gardner (Harvard).
Multiple intelligences	(3) This deals with the physical, social and emotional conditions within which learning is optimized. It is based on the explosion of neuroscientific findings in the mid-to-late 1980s.
Brain-based learning	(4) Driven by the notion that human brains have tremendous capacity and that full potential can never be realized. No one has a fixed level of intelligence, and under the right conditions each student is able to become cleverer. The concept of IQ goes out of the window!

Drawing learning theory and practice together within the classroom is invariably the focus of the first subject-based assignment. You may be asked to explore and analyse critically a range of learning theories or the most appropriate one to your own subject area. On some courses you will be required to reflect upon your own development in the light of these theories, or asked to consider how they are applied and adapted in the classroom context. How you achieve this and its value in terms of your professional development are discussed in more detail in Chapters 3, 4 and 5 but for now, consider the emphasis underpinning such an assignment:

 Secondary science PGCE M-level

The first assignment, entitled 'Curriculum developments in science', has three essential strands. The first is simply an opportunity to focus on a concept or idea from the Key Stage 3 curriculum and to map it both backwards to Key Stages 1 and 2 and forwards through Key Stage 4 in order to gain some appreciation of how the chosen topic is developed. This provides a means of engagement with the secondary science curriculum including the development of some understanding of the range of options and routes through Key Stage 4.

The second strand requires an exploration of some educational research. Initially this will be promoted by looking at a constructivist view of learning (often used in science education) although the literature search may be expanded to other areas of interest. Linked examples would be to include a view of likely misconceptions linked to the chosen topic, or perhaps to research how to motivate pupils successfully so that they are open to further developing their science knowledge.

The third part of the assignment involves the students carrying out some practitioner research at their first placement school. This aspect of the assignment has been left fairly open so that the students can use it to pursue their own interests in the context of the widely differing schools that they will experience. The most successful students will 'knit' these three strands together to produce an assignment where the links between learning theory, practice in their placement school and their own developing practice are explored in the context of one aspect of the science curriculum.

A big part of the learning process is being able to demonstrate what you have learnt and how you can use it. This is accessed through the assessment process, but over the years assessment has tended to dictate the content and style of teaching. We will always need to externalize what we know in order to gauge the effectiveness of the learning process, but there needs to be a sense of ownership associated with this. The learner is, however, central to the learning process and therefore needs to be at the helm steering this process in the most appropriate direction. To achieve this the learner, whether it is you or the pupils you teach, must reflect upon their own learning, constantly assessing the information coming in and the impact it is having on achieving the desirable goals. This is seldom achieved alone; it usually requires expert scaffolding from the teacher and supporting peers.

The importance of a learning community, one which supports and enables its members through the learning process, has long been recognized. Establishment of such a community may be formally developed, i.e. a short/medium-term group work activity, or informally developed, i.e. your own PGCE group of peers who meet regularly outside the formal sessions. Communication may be face-to-face or via some electronic means, i.e. through a purpose-built virtual learning site such as Blackboard or WebCT, or possibly through Facebook. However, several ground rules are important:

- Membership of the group is limited to those involved in the activity in hand and may include an academic tutor in a peripatetic capacity.

- The main task of the group is 'learning' related.

- Opportunities for each member to have their say followed by open discussion must be made available.

- General group dynamics invariably apply, but for effective learning to take place each member and their comments must feel valued.

Activity: Thinking about communities of learning (1)

Identify at least three opportunities when you have had to work collaboratively in a learning situation.

- Do you feel you work well in a group? *Justify your answer.*
- What do you consider to be the benefits of working collaboratively?
- What reservations do you have about this approach to learning?

 Activity: Thinking about communities of learning (2)

Consider the four bullet points on the previous page. Discuss with your peers how these could be established effectively in the following situations:

- your PGCE cohort;
- within a school class;
- virtually, through some electronic means.

What potential problems could you foresee with the virtual situation?

From the learner's perspective the ability to reflect upon one's own learning has become widely recognized within teaching and learning (Fisher, 1995; Bruner, 1996; Parker and Hess, 2001; Maiteny, 2002; Pollard, 2002; Ward and McCotter, 2004; Lakin, 2005). The effectiveness of this process, however, appears to depend upon the level of reflection administered. A child at Key Stage 2 can reflect upon their own level of knowledge and understanding and possibly suggest in simple terms what they would need to do to progress to the next level of attainment. Likewise a child in Key Stages 3 and 4, but at what stage does this cease being the superficial 'explain something rather than describe it' to form the more detailed progression leading to conceptual change? To achieve conceptual change, with or without the input of an expert practitioner, the learner needs to be actively engaged in the learning process. This goes beyond the mere inclusion of active learning activities. As Ross et al. explain, 'active learning doesn't usually give autonomy over organization of the learning to the learner: many active learning tasks are very directional and specific, but the main point is that they are impossible to do unless the pupils *think*' (2004: 58). But what do we understand by 'thinking' and how can it be effective?

Activity

Discuss the following questions with a group of your peers:

- Is thinking a 'higher-order' activity?
- Is thinking a 'skill' that can be taught and learnt? Can it be broken down into progressive steps that can be taught?
- Is thinking context dependent?
- How could you promote thinking-centred learning?

For the learning process to be productive, time is required for the learner to reformulate the ideas they are inputting, to assimilate them and take ownership of them. Until this happens the learner's engagement is only superficial, and deep learning (the acquisition of higher-order skills such as analysing, interpreting and evaluating information rather than simply amassing, reproducing and describing it) is not achieved (Hill and Woodland, 2002). As mentioned earlier, part of this process is to recognize and fill the gaps in subject knowledge and understanding. If the learner has the ability to tease out conceptual progression, identifying the stages in the development of a concept, for example density or photosynthesis, gaps in the subject knowledge may begin to appear. For example, what do I need to know to progress from understanding that a green plant requires sunlight, 'air' and water to survive, to understanding, and indeed explaining, that it is a combination of carbon dioxide and oxygen that is needed, along with other requirements, for a plant to survive.

Summary

In this chapter we have explored the significance of taking ownership for one's learning and how this can contribute to a more effective learning process. We have also discussed how it is possible for you as a teacher to play a significant role in that process by ensuring that your own SKU continues to develop and by applying a range of well-selected and appropriate learning approaches to address the variety of learning needs within the classroom. How this contributes to your own long-term development as a reflective practitioner is discussed further in Chapter 3.

Suggestions and answers to activities

Threshold concepts: opportunity costs

Economists have a particular interest in how we make decisions. The concept of 'opportunity costs' is one that considers all the alternative opportunities and the value we place on them. The idea is far removed from the predetermined 'no choice in the matter' perspective, towards a more abstract view of decision-making which recognizes and values the idea that every alternative has two sides to it, each supported by value-laden consequences. Meyer and Land (2003) explain that the 'opportunity cost' is the evaluation attributed to the most highly valued of the rejected alternatives. Once a person assumes this view they have made significant progress in their thinking and decision-making.

Threshold concepts: dinosaurs

Evidence suggests that the dinosaurs were around for approximately 260 million years. When they first evolved the continents were united in a super-continent called Pangaea. The sections that would later become Europe and America were indistinguishable and the early dinosaurs that inhabited Pangaea could indeed walk from what would be Europe to what would be America. Towards the end of the dinosaurs' reign, the super-continent divided and the landmasses separated and moved north, eventually forming a new arrangement similar to that of today. The two subcontinents were now separated by the Atlantic Ocean, making it impossible for the dinosaurs to travel between continents. This question is about the nature of the Earth's crust, based on evidence supporting the theory of plate tectonics. An understanding of this paves the way to a more dynamic understanding of the makeup of the Earth, its geology and its biodiversity.

Identify some threshold concepts in your own subject area, explaining why they adhere to this description.

Pedagogy

Table 2.3 shows the possible influencing factors in the learning environment.

Table 2.3 Possible influencing factors in the learning environment

Learner	Peers	Teacher	Teaching assistants
Age	Group selection and dynamics	Biography	How informed they are about the lesson
Socio-democratic standing	Learning stage of group members		Biography
Learning stage	SEN		

Table 2.4 shows the suggested responses to the problem posed in Table 2.1.

Table 2.4 Answers to Table 2.1

Theories and approaches	Definition
Co-constructed learning	(3)
Accelerated learning	(1)
Differentiated learning	(8) – This approach is linked to the current drive for personalized learning and has implications for inclusion. Find out more about the terms 'gifted and talented' and 'challenged' in the context of learners' individual needs.
Constructivism	(6)
Learning to learn and meta-learning	(2) – Meta-learning is the reflective element of this.
Thinking skills and metacognition	(7) – Find out more about CASE and P4C and how they can be incorporated in your own teaching. Metacognition is the process, but what are the five categories of thinking skills?

| Assessment for learning | (4) – There are a number of associated techniques, such as clarifying and communicating learning outcomes, self- and peer-assessment, the use of no-hands-up policy, probing questioning by the teacher and no grading or numerical marking of the students' work. |
| Personalized learning | (5) – Hargreaves (2004) has proposed nine 'gateways' to personalized learning, creating a framework which pulls together many current initiatives. Find out more about these. |

Table 2.5 shows the correct responses to the problem posed in Table 2.2.

Table 2.5 Answers to Table 2.2

Learning style, construct or model	Definition
Learnable intelligence	(4) – The concept of IQ goes out of the window!
Emotional intelligence	(1)
Multiple intelligences	(2) – At least eight discrete intelligences have been identified that every person has to differing degrees. Find out what they are and if there are any additional ones identified elsewhere.
Brain-based learning	(3) – Made possible by new brain-scanning technologies.

Activity on community of learning (1)

Learning communities can be very effective, with each member bringing their own experiences, values and perspectives to the community. All members work within the same framework, established either formally or informally. Such practices can be very helpful in 'problem-solving' scenarios or when considering challenges. Some people, however, feel less comfortable or confident with collaboration, preferring to work independently. There could be problems of group dynamics and disagreements over particular matters. For the community to work well and the members to fully benefit, these dynamics need to be addressed. This is not always an easy task, but one that must be recognized.

Activity on community of learning (2)

The use of the virtual learning environment (e.g. WebCT, Blackboard, Moogle, *Glow*) are well established in most schools and universities. Successfully learning through these media varies considerably but the benefits are worth considering. Often not set in real time, members of the learning community can access and contribute to the discussion at their convenience; to be fully effective this needs formalizing and monitoring. Issues of dynamics and especially e-etiquette apply, equally in a virtual community as in a face-to-face one, and need agreed protocols and monitoring. Despite the accessibility advantages of a vehicle such as Facebook for establishing chat rooms and discussion areas, the open-access nature of this forum can prohibit its effectiveness as a desired learning environment.

Activity on thinking

Researchers in the USA (Watkins, 2006) have concluded that thinking isn't a higher-order activity, nor is it a skill. It can't be subdivided into convenient components but it is context-dependent. How do these answers compare with your own and how might this inform and influence your own practice? Watkins suggests that 'thinking-centred learning' is pupil-driven and discussion-centred, where problem-solving is encouraged but relevant and pupils are asked to demonstrate their methodology and, hence, understanding. Alternative views and 'what-if' scenarios are included to encourage creativity and critical analysis.

 In search of Aira Force *or* How not to climb Helvellyn

Prior to writing the second edition of this book, I revisited this walk to Aira Force. With the hindsight of the above experience and some careful preparation I arrived at the 'correct' car park and soon realized how all the signs and waymarkers indicated on the 'easy walks' guide fitted into place. This emphasized the importance of reflecting and revisiting practice. We cannot hope to get things 'right' the first time, as discussed earlier there are so many variants and influences contributing to the way we first encounter something. We do, however, have the **potential** to analyse and question our experiences and it is this potential that as teachers we need to develop and hone in our pupils, whatever our subject specialism and whatever age group we teach.

📖 Further reading

Bryan, H., Carpenter, C. and Hoult, S. (2010) *Learning and Teaching at M-Level*. London: Sage. The notion of how critical thinking underpins the developing professional is a key focus of this book.

Driscoll, P., Lambirth, J. and Roden, A. (eds) (2011) *The Primary Curriculum: A Creative Approach*. London: Sage. This book provides a useful overview of the primary curriculum along with guidance on how to develop a creative approach to teaching and learning.

Driver, R., Guesne, E. and Tiberghien, A. (eds) (1985) *Children's Ideas in Science*. Milton Keynes: Open University Press. This book provides a useful insight into scientific learning and the development of concepts and misconceptions.

Ellis, V. (ed.) (2011) *Learning and Teaching in Secondary Schools*, 4th edn. Exeter: Learning Matters. This is a useful text for developing an understanding of the ways in which research and theory underpin progress in the professional standards for trainee secondary teachers.

Fautley, M. and Savage, J. (2010) *Secondary Education, Reflective Reader*. Exeter: Learning Matters. A useful reflective reader which explores the relationship between theory, research and practice through key themes in secondary education.

Hayes, D. (2004) *Foundations of Primary Teaching*. 3rd edn. London: David Fulton. A very useful book to explore a range of aspects associated with working as a primary teacher.

Judge, B., Jones, P. and McCreery, E. (2010) *Critical Thinking for Education Students*. Exeter: Learning Matters. A useful text for helping trainee teachers to understand critical analysis and the use of data in developing teaching approaches.

References

Bennett, J. (2003) *Teaching and Learning Science: A Guide to Recent Research and Its Application*. London: Continuum.

Bruner, J. (1996) *The Culture of Education*. London: Harvard University Press.

DfEE and QCA (1999) *The National Curriculum for England*. London: HMSO.

Fisher, R. (1995) *Teaching Children to Think*. Cheltenham: Stanley Thornes.

Gardner, H. (1985) *Frames of Mind: The Theory of Multiple Intelligences*. London: Paladin Books.

Hargreaves, D. (2004) *Personalised Learning: Next Steps in Working Laterally*. Online at: http://www.clusterweb.org.uk/docs/hargreavespersonalisedlearning.pdf.

Hill, J. and Woodland, W. (2002) 'An evaluation of foreign fieldwork in promoting deep learning: a preliminary investigation', *Assessment and Evaluation in Higher Education*, 27 (6): 530–55.

Kyriacou, C. (1998) *Essential Teaching Skills*, 2nd edn. Cheltenham: Stanley Thornes.

Lakin, L. (2005) 'Developing innovative pedagogy to enhance teaching and learning in science and environmental education', *Research in Teacher Education*, 5: 397–402.

McGuinness, C. (1999) *Thinking Skills to Thinking Classrooms*. Belfast: Queen's University.

Maiteny, P. (2002) 'Mind the gap: summary of research exploring "inner" influences on pro-sustainability learning and behaviour', *Environmental Education Research*, 8 (3): 299–306.

Meyer, J. and Land, R. (2003) *Threshold Concepts and Troublesome Knowledge: Linkages to Ways of Thinking and Practising Within Disciplines*. Edinburgh: ETL Projects, TLRP.

Parker, W. and Hess, D. (2001) 'Teaching with and for discussion', *Teaching and Teacher Education*, 17: 273–89.

Pollard, A. (2002) *Reflective Teaching: Effective and Evidence-Informed Professional Practice*. London: Continuum.

Ross, K., Lakin, L. and Callaghan, P. (2004) *Teaching Secondary Science*, 2nd edn. London: David Fulton.

Schunk, D.H. (1996) *Learning Theories*, 2nd edn. Englewood Cliffs, NJ: Prentice Hall.

TDA (Training and Development Agency for Schools) (2007) *Professional Standards for Teachers*. London: TDA. (NB: These standards apply only in England.)

Ward, J. and McCotter, S. (2004) 'Reflection as a visible outcome for pre-service teachers', *Teaching and Teacher Education*, 20: 243–57.

Watkins, C. (2006) *Learning: A Sense-maker's Guide*. London: ATL.

3 What can I expect my PGCE at M-level to look like during my school-based training?

Alex Woodgate-Jones

This chapter aims to help you understand what doing a PGCE at M-level will involve during your school-based training. In order to do this, it will explore:

- the role of reflection and reflective practice, as this is where you will demonstrate that you are working at M-level;

- the different stages that you may go through in developing your reflective skills;

- the role of your mentor in supporting you to develop reflective skills.

Context

A period of time spent in 'real-life classrooms' has always played a part in the training of teachers. The length of time spent in schools as part of PGCE courses has changed over the years and it is only in comparatively recent times that the amount of time trainees must spend on school-based training (SBT) has increased dramatically. Now, on a secondary PGCE course, trainees must normally spend a minimum of 24 weeks and on a primary PGCE, 18 weeks. Considering that a PGCE course usually lasts 38 weeks, the school-based training element represents a significant component. Because of the increased duration of SBT, its role has changed and evolved. In the past, it was often said that trainees went to initial teacher education (ITE) institutions to learn about the theory but they went into schools to learn the practice; the two were seen as completely different entities, with theory and practice bearing little relation to each other. Indeed this is sometimes still said today. However, in order to complete a PGCE at M-level, the theory/practice gap must be bridged. Teacher education takes place in both schools and ITE institutions. Schools provide teacher education, not only practical experiences, and, in the same way, ITE institutions do not just provide 'unrealistic' theories. The aim is that all aspects of the PGCE course work together so that you will leave the course as a reflective practitioner, able to take responsibility for your own further professional development. This chapter aims to explore the role SBT plays in the PGCE at Masters level, focusing particularly on the skills of critical reflection as a vehicle to do this.

In the last two decades terms such as *reflective practitioner, reflective teaching* and *the critically reflective teacher* have been widely used in the field of education. The general idea underpinning all these has been for teachers to be more thoughtful and critically analytical about their practice. Teachers are now encouraged to be action researchers, self-analysers, problem-solvers and innovators, in addition to the narrower view of teaching often perceived by those not in the profession. Your friends and family who don't teach may well think that teaching is simply a matter of passing on facts and telling classes of pupils what to do! As explained in Chapter 1, the notion of professionalism has evolved in recent years and it is now commonly accepted that the 'tips for teachers' approach to ITE is not sufficient in preparing you to deliver a diverse and creative curriculum. This development should be seen as a positive move towards valuing the profession of teaching, but only if the idea of reflection is applied in a practical way. If we are not careful, the word 'reflection' could just become the latest buzzword: an idea that is given lip service and used in application forms and job interviews to show we are at the cutting edge of education! I am sure you will have come across these or similar terms already, but what do they actually mean?

What exactly is reflection?

First we need to explore what reflection actually is and where it comes from. It is often assumed that we all mean the same thing when we talk about 'reflection' but this is not necessarily the case. There are many different interpretations and so I would like to go back to the beginning, to where the idea originally came from. It was proposed by John Dewey (an American philosopher, psychologist and educational reformer) in 1933. He contrasted 'routine action' with 'reflective action' and he went on to develop what he called the reflective phases. These consist of *suggestions–problem–hypothesis–reasoning–testing*. These phases may not necessarily occur in the order suggested and, as in the model presented in Figure 3.1, testing may not be the end of the cycle as you may then need to develop further suggestions.

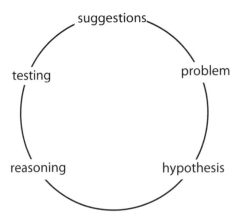

Figure 3.1 The reflective phases

I will explain what these might look like for you while on SBT a little later in the chapter. As a working definition I would like you to think of reflection as involving a thoughtful examination of your own practice, based on your analysis of the successful practice of others, and research findings, including your own research in your own classrooms (action research). Once you have analysed a particular aspect of your practice and considered ways of improving it you will then apply that understanding to your practice and continue the process. As you can see, it is a complex, cyclical process and it is not enough to simply think about an aspect of your teaching. The important thing to bear in mind here is that reflection should be productive and progress is achieved by actually changing your practice as a result of reflection. It should be noted, however, that although there is a relationship between research and classroom practice I am not suggesting that you take all research findings and apply them unquestioningly in your classroom. You will always need to use your professional judgement to effectively interpret the findings and evaluate the significance and reliability of the research evidence. This is another example of how the university-based elements of the PGCE M-level course dovetail with the SBT element.

So how can I develop my reflective skills and what is my role in this process?

Most importantly, you must remember that you are an active participant in your own training and development. The PGCE course (and all that it entails) is not something that happens *to* you, implying that you are a passive recipient of training. Instead, you should consider yourself to be an active partner, responsible for your own learning and shaping your own progress.

This might sound rather daunting if you are just beginning your PGCE course, as you will already be juggling a number of new ideas/commitments, but don't panic! You will not be expected to be critically reflective the moment you start teaching. You will probably find that you need to build up your confidence in the day-to-day management initially before you can move on to self-evaluation and critical reflection. However, you can begin this process by analysing your own perceptions of teaching and learning.

 Activity

Consider what your perceptions of teaching and learning are. Where do these perceptions come from? You will probably have spent some time in schools as preparation for your PGCE course and so a useful starting point would be to examine how schools today differ from your experience of school as a pupil. For example, are teaching styles similar/different, how is discipline maintained, is the organization the same/different, are extra-curricular activities similar, and so on.

It is generally accepted that most trainees go through several different stages during their SBT. The following are based on stages proposed by Furlong and Maynard (1995).

Stage 1: Idealism

Students are often highly idealistic before training begins, identifying closely with the pupils. This is obviously something which should continue to underpin your practice throughout your teaching career but it can quickly fade once you are in the classroom setting.

Stage 2: Survival

At this stage you might feel as though there is just too much to remember and cope with. It is important for you to focus on the things you can do successfully rather than become bogged down by those you have not yet mastered. On the other hand, if you are doing a lot of observation, an experienced teacher can make everything seem very easy and simple and you may not understand the complex processes at work. Consider the example of James in the following case study.

LIBRARY, UNIVERSITY C CHESTER

Case study

James has just completed a two-week introductory placement in a primary school. In his first taught session at university there was a discussion about the trainees' experiences in schools, which focused on teachers' behaviour management. He shared his experience of having been in a particular class for a week where the pupils were very well behaved. At this point he had presumed that the class was 'easy'. In the following week the teacher was away for the morning and a supply teacher was covering the lessons. He was amazed to see how the pupils' behaviour deteriorated. It became clear to him that, in fact, it was the class teacher's effective behaviour management strategies that made the class appear easy to teach rather than the class being naturally well behaved. Until he observed the supply teacher, he was unaware of the strategies the teacher was using to positively manage the pupils' behaviour. They were invisible to him because they were working so well. He has now begun to reflect on exactly what is going on and what the teacher is doing to make things run smoothly.

It is notoriously difficult to dissect exactly what a teacher is doing as there are so many things going on at the same time. You almost have to know what you're looking for to be able to see it.

Stage 3: Dealing with problems

The focus for reflection here will depend on the challenges you are facing. The trick is to try to disentangle the complex processes you are seeing in practice and identify some of the difficulties involved. It may be tempting at this stage to try to copy the teacher but unless you understand why certain strategies work and why the teacher has chosen them, this will not stand you in good stead for future progress.

 Case study

Take Jaspal, a secondary PE trainee who was struggling to manage his Year 9 class. He spent several lessons observing his subject mentor, focusing particularly on the mentor's use of praise to encourage pupils to follow his instructions. Jaspal then taught a lesson in which he attempted to employ the same strategy, but found it much less successful than when his mentor did it. Jaspal had fallen into the trap of simply copying a strategy without fully understanding what had made it effective. After a discussion with his university-based tutor he was able to reflect on why this had happened. The tutor helped Jaspal unpick the principles underpinning the use of praise: for example, that praise should be specific, well timed and genuine, and that different pupils respond to praise differently depending on how it is given. Having reflected on this and compared it to his earlier attempts, he was then able (with the support of his mentor) to apply this to his following lessons to much greater effect.

Stage 4: Plateauing

Once a student has mastered the basics of running the class, sometimes they hit a plateau. At this stage it is helpful for the reflection to focus on the pupils' learning rather than solely on the teaching. With support, it is important for you not to become complacent but to continue to analyse and strive to make improvements to your practice.

 Case study

Amelia serves as a good example of this. She was in the middle of a successful placement and had just been observed by her mentor. In Amelia's mind, the lesson had gone without a hitch. The pupils had done what she'd asked of them and appeared to enjoy the lesson. The timings had worked out well and transitions were well managed. She was therefore taken aback to find that during the feedback her mentor was not overly complimentary. She asked Amelia to consider the amount of progress the pupils had made during the lesson. Amelia's initial reaction was surprise and disappointment. However, during the course of the discussion she realized she had been focusing too much on classroom management as a sign of effective teaching at the expense of the pupils' learning. Through this critical reflection she was able to develop her practice to take more account of the learning that was going on as well as her teaching.

This example clearly shows how continuous reflection avoids plateauing and leads to more effective teaching and learning.

Stage 5: Moving on

As you gain in confidence, you can take increasing responsibility for your own development. Reflection continues to play a pivotal role in this, as students broaden their teaching strategies as well as begin to consider the wider implications of education (including social, moral and political dimensions). At this stage you should be looking for challenges and initiating your own reflection.

Case study

Zhen was in her final placement and had identified a number of pupils who appeared not to be actively engaged in her lessons as an area that needed improving. She had attended taught sessions at university about learning theories, how to motivate pupils and how to incorporate different learning styles in the classroom. She had also read some recently published research articles about how pupils learn and the benefits of group work. In her time spent observing other teachers' practice, Zhen had noted down specific strategies related to involving all pupils in their lessons. She had been working in this particular class for four weeks and had built up a good relationship with them. Using all her knowledge and experience she identified some strategies in an attempt to encourage more pupils to be actively involved in her lessons. These included adopting a 'no hands up' policy and planning more activities that involved pupils working collaboratively in groups. She taught in this way for the following week and then asked her mentor for a focused observation to judge the effectiveness of these strategies. As a result, she chose to continue to include these approaches in her teaching. However, during this time she also observed a knock-on effect. She had thought that the use of groups would increase the engagement of all the pupils in the class, but having tried it she found that some group-work activities highlighted the issue of the more dominant characters taking over with the less confident pupils playing a minor role. She concluded from this that the group-work strategy had potential but that she needed to manage the group dynamics better.

Here we see an example of the complex and cyclical nature of effective reflection as outlined by Dewey. Once Zhen had identified the problem, made her hypothesis, thought it through and tested it out, she realized she had to go round again and make a new hypothesis, thus repeating the cycle. According to the Quality Assurance Agency (2001), M-level trainees should make sure their practice is informed by current theory and research at the forefront of primary education. The way Zhen reflected on her practice, consulted others and read up on the latest research findings shows she is clearly working at this level.

At this point it is important to consider the dangers of seeing these stages as representing a linear model of progression. This is not the case. Progression will probably not happen in such a neat way: sometimes you may stay at the same stage for a long time and then suddenly make a leap forward, at other times you may well consider yourself to have moved from one stage to another only to find that in order to make further progress you have to go backwards to go forwards. Let me explain using an example. Imagine that a trainee has found that through shouting they are able to manage the behaviour of pupils in the class. This is not a desirable sustainable strategy and so in order to progress and develop other behaviour management strategies, the shouting approach has to be unlearned and other approaches incorporated. During this time, while the trainee is working out which other strategies work for them, their behaviour management might be perceived as having got worse. This is only temporary, as once the trainee has developed a wider range of strategies, they will be in a position to make much more progress. So we can see that going through the stages is much more haphazard than it might at first appear.

How should I record the process of reflection?

Different PGCE courses will vary in the formats they suggest trainees use to show evidence of reflection. Many institutions will encourage you to keep a diary or journal. This can be completed at the end of each day or week to record your reflections and observations. Writing a journal or diary in this way can help you untangle themes that otherwise might seem jumbled. It is also a very useful tool for identifying your key issues, and may help you move from one stage of reflection to the next. For example, you may find when reading your journal that most of your reflections are based on your teaching style or behaviour management strategies. This could alert you to the fact that you may need to spend more time considering the learning going on in the class.

Lesson evaluations are also key in encouraging and demonstrating reflection. Consider the following case studies of the same lesson from the perspective of two different trainees:

 Kate's lesson evaluation

The lesson went quite well. I think most pupils understood the learning objective. Each part of the lesson lasted about the right amount of time. All the pupils finished the task although some might have been copying each other. Next time I'll sit them further apart.

Targets: Change the seating arrangements.

 Sam's lesson observation

There were several aspects of the lesson I was pleased with. The pupils definitely understood the learning objective and came up with some really good success criteria. All the pupils finished the task but I should have differentiated it more because Samirah, Paul, Lucy and Nasir finished it really quickly (remember to plan more opportunities for pupils to engage with open-ended investigations). Jack, Amy and Sarah struggled and started copying the others (a word bank would have been useful to support their learning). I am pleased that my attempts to increase the pace of my introductions are beginning to work. Next time I would like feedback on the ratio of teacher-talk to pupil-talk during the introduction.

Targets: Differentiation: consider ways of supporting the lower-attaining pupils (provide resources/practical supports). Think about extending the higher-attaining pupils (open-ended investigations). Encourage more interaction during the introduction (more open questioning).

Activity

From these two evaluations, how would you answer the following questions:

- What have Kate and Sam understood about the pupils' learning?
- On what evidence have they based their judgements?
- To what extent have they unpicked the issues that arose?
- How useful are their lesson evaluations in terms of helping them improve their practice?

It is clear that the reflection in Sam's lesson evaluation is at a much higher level than Kate's. You could say that they have both identified the same issue of the copying, but rather than seeing this as the pupils' fault (as Kate has done), Sam has considered what might have caused them to do this, that is, he is trying to analyse the underlying reasons. Having done this, he has decided that it was due to the pupils not feeling able to do the task and has planned to address this by differentiating it more. Kate is also rather vague about who was doing the copying, whereas Sam has identified exactly which pupils were doing this. Kate has merely seen the behaviour and decided to act on that by separating all the pupils more, which will not solve the problem in the long term. Unfortunately Kate has also based her judgements about whether the pupils understood the learning objective on a 'feeling' rather than on any evidence. While she may be correct in this assumption, without any evidence to back it up she could equally as easily be mistaken. Sam knows the pupils understood the learning objective in his lesson because he asked them to devise success criteria to show that.

Sam's targets are also much more helpful than Kate's. They are focused, specific and help the mentor to help him by identifying exactly what he would like to happen next (i.e. taking responsibility for his own learning). After his next lessons he will be able to reflect on whether these strategies proved successful, whereas Kate will only see how pupils cope with tasks on their own. She will then have to start the process of analysing potential reasons if they fail to manage them. However, judging from her first lesson evaluation she may well not be ready to do this without support from her mentor/tutor. Sam is already functioning at a much higher level and is developing the skill of critical reflection.

You may find that your ITE institution has set specific directed activities to complete while on SBT. These are designed to help you begin to ask questions which will lead you to reflect on your or others' practice. Here is an example of an activity you may be asked to carry out during your first period of SBT.

Reflective Activity

Decide on one aspect which you will focus on to evaluate a lesson. This could be learning in a specific subject, addressing misconceptions, behaviour management, use of ICT, etc. When planning, identify what you want this aspect of the lesson to achieve. For example, if you chose ICT did you want it to motivate learners, promote learning, help manage behaviour, etc? Having taught your lesson, evaluate your chosen aspect against what you had intended: what worked well, what didn't work so well, and how do you know? Write down the things which you have identified as indicators of success (or otherwise). Hopefully one of these will be about learning but how do you know that learning has taken place? What information do you need to support this?

Organize your evaluation in four boxes:

- What did the children learn?
- Next steps in children's learning
- How effective was your teaching?
- How will you modify/change your teaching as a result?

Looking particularly at the final question, what reading do you need to do in order to support your development? What do you know already? What do you need to know? Remember that your thinking should focus on the theories underpinning how children learn.

Directed activity example

In negotiation with your class teacher, plan to teach the same group, in the same subject, for two consecutive lessons.

- Plan your teaching input, thinking carefully about how you will share with the pupils what is to be learned (*learning objectives*) and what they will be expected to be able to do when they have learned it (*success criteria*).

- During the teaching session and afterwards, begin to work on strategies to check on pupils' understanding, for example through questioning, observing, discussing, pupil review and analysing pupils' verbal or written responses.

- Feed back your observations to the class teacher – ideally with a brief written record (formats can be devised or borrowed).

- Evaluate your lesson, identifying the next teaching step for the group and reflecting on the effectiveness of the lesson and how you have involved the pupils in evaluating their own learning. What would you do differently next time?

- Plan, teach and evaluate the next lesson in close liaison with your class teacher.

This particular activity is designed to support you in developing your understanding of the planning, teaching, assessing cycle while working with a small group. Once completed, you take your notes back to the ITE institution and discuss the findings and implications in taught sessions. You then need to reflect on this discussion and make informed decisions which impact on your practice on the next period of SBT. In this way the close relationship between SBT and the ITE institution is explicit. This example also serves to highlight how your tutors and mentors will help you develop the skills required for reflection; they will not expect you to be able to do it on your own, without support. The help you receive will take a variety of forms, and the mentor plays a key role in this. As there is sometimes confusion over what mentoring actually entails, I would like to outline the role of the mentor.

The role of the mentor

Although some ITE institutions and schools may use a different term, the 'mentor' is the person who supports and monitors your progress while you are in school. In secondary schools you may have a generic mentor who looks after all the students in the school and also a subject-specific mentor who monitors your day-to-day subject teaching. In addition you will be allocated a tutor from your training institution who will work in partnership with you and the school to support your overall training. Whatever this person is called, your relationship with your mentor is paramount to a successful SBT, on both personal and professional levels.

It is not necessary to become best friends with your mentor, but you must endeavour to establish an open and trusting relationship with them. They will play a key role in helping you shape and develop your reflective skills. This may seem perfectly obvious and I am sure you will have every intention of doing this. There are some specific things you can do, apart from relying on your personal charm! Most importantly you should appear open-minded, enthusiastic and keen to learn. Remember that it is not only you that may be feeling nervous about your SBT. Your class-based mentor may also be feeling apprehensive. After all, you will be observing them teach, and if they are not overly experienced they may be worried about how they will manage their role as a mentor. It is not as simple as watching each other teach with the mentor then passing on some tips. Mentors will vary enormously in terms of their experience, training and approach; it is up to you to make sure you get the kind of support you need. Obviously there may be times when this is not possible, but generally you can be as proactive in this area as you would be in any other.

As stated earlier, you should not assume that your mentor is as comfortable with you observing them teach as they may appear or as you imagine them to be. Therefore you should approach this task in the same way as you would expect them to approach their observation of you, once you have started teaching. In order to get the most out of lesson observations, here are some useful things to bear in mind.

Before the lesson:

- Agree on when and how the observation will take place. Clarify what your role in it will be; for example, will you observe from a detached viewpoint, or will you get involved and help the pupils?

- Find out as much background information as possible. How does the lesson fit in with prior learning/subsequent plans, what are the teacher's aims, are there any pupils with particular needs?

- Open, unfocused observations are vague and of little value. In consultation with your mentor, agree a focus on one or two areas, for example behaviour management, assessment strategies, questioning, beginnings/endings of lessons.

- Agree a time for discussion afterwards. This is essential to develop reflective understanding. There is little point in observation without discussion. This should take place fairly soon after the lesson but not necessarily immediately – within 24 hours is normally suggested.

During the lesson:

- Even if you do not agree with the practice you are observing, you should try to analyse and reflect on why the teacher may have acted in a particular way before coming to any conclusions. Remember, you are there to learn from a more experienced practitioner.

After the lesson:

- Try to ask open-ended questions which will encourage the teacher to explain in more depth their reasons for using a particular strategy.

- Do not appear to criticize (it is useful to phrase questions with 'Why did you . . . ?' rather than 'Why didn't you . . . ?').

- Write down key points so that you remember the main issues that arose and can reflect on them.

- Thank the teacher.

This is very similar to the way a mentor will organize their observations of your teaching (although they may not thank you!).

It is absolutely essential to build in time for feedback after a lesson observation. This is an opportunity for some joint reflection to take place. During this time your mentor can really help you focus your reflections. They will probably ask you questions such as:

- How do you think the lesson went?

- What were you pleased with?

- What was the aim of the lesson?

- What did the pupils learn?

- Why did you choose that particular activity?

- Did anything go differently (i.e. better or worse) from how you expected it to?

- If you taught the lesson again would you do anything differently?

- What will you do in the next lesson?

- How can you now move forward?

If you find yourself in a position where your mentor is not asking you these questions, you should ask them of yourself and include your responses in your diary or lesson evaluations. Once you are into your SBT and feel more confident you could also make these questions more general, and ask yourself the following (based on Fletcher, 2000):

- What do I do well?

- How can I do it even better?

- What needs improving?

- What can I do to improve it?

- Can I do it on my own or do I need help?

- How will I know if it is improving?

This follows the definition of reflection outlined at the beginning of the chapter. By asking and answering these questions, you will be analysing your practice, identifying problem areas, devising an intervention designed to solve the problem and then trying it out (just as Dewey suggested in his five phases: *suggestions–problem–hypothesis–reasoning–testing*). This model can make it sound as though these phases are neatly packaged and that one simply follows on from the other. This is definitely not the case; although they may appear sequential, they are not intended to be interpreted in this way. The phases will often overlap and will feel a lot messier than this model makes it appear. As a user-friendly approach, you may want to bear in mind the 'plan, do, review' teaching strategy. This is used primarily in the Reception year but can easily be applied to the domain of critical reflection.

It is important to note at this point that class-based mentors may well not make explicit links to research findings when supporting mentees in developing the skills of critical reflection. This is because they are more likely to use their own experience and make decisions based on research they have carried out in their own classrooms. Let us look at the example of Elena, an experienced secondary teacher and mentor.

 Case study

In all the schools Elena has worked in during her career so far, it has been a requirement to set a certain amount of homework. However, she began to have concerns that the homework she was setting was not interesting to the pupils or supporting their learning. Rather, it had become a time-consuming chore that pupils could see little point in completing. She also felt that from her point of view she was setting it in order to 'tick the box'. So she decided to go back to the school policy which talked about the aim of homework being to 'consolidate and extend learning'. With this in mind she set about changing the style of the homework she set to make it more relevant to this aim. First she started setting homework that was more directly linked to the lesson it followed on from and, in addition, she built the homework into the following lesson. This meant that the homework had to be done in order for the class to tackle the next lesson. She was pleased to find that the pupils were more motivated, and as an added bonus she found she did less marking as there were more opportunities for self- and peer-assessment. Having reflected on this process she is now considering giving the class more ownership of their homework by allowing them to choose how they present their work.

Although Elena may not consider herself to have carried out action research (according to the 'official' definition used in academic research literature), there are many similarities. It certainly shows her to be a critically reflective practitioner and her findings are of no less value to you as a trainee than published research findings. As a trainee you will start off relying on research that others have undertaken and it is important to remember that whatever form the research may take this in no way diminishes its relevance. As a trainee working at M-level you should be reflecting on teaching and learning in your classroom, consulting current theory and research findings, applying them where appropriate in your classroom, reflecting on their effectiveness and even further developing innovations.

If the mentoring and reflection process is working successfully, it should be cyclical. You should be able to: discuss the focus of the lesson observation with your mentor – have the observation – have a discussion – set targets (in consultation with your mentor) – and then begin the cycle again. I would like to re-emphasize here the role you, as the trainee, play in this. You should hopefully be taking the initiative in the discussion and looking to suggest your own targets. Through reflection you should have prepared what you feel you need to talk about before you have the meeting. Just as when you are teaching you encourage pupils to take ownership of their own learning, the mentor's aim is to scaffold your thinking and guide you to solve your own difficulties, rather than simply telling you what to do. In order for this model to work, you must remember that being challenged by a mentor is not intended to be a personal attack but rather a way of supporting learning. It is therefore your responsibility to be ready to receive advice and enter this type of critically reflective discussion openly. You may become concerned about taking up too much of the mentor's time and asking too much of them. This should be taken into consideration to a certain extent (if you are expecting them to sit down with you every day after school for several hours!) but it is not all a one-way street.

What does my mentor get out of it?

A mentor should not see taking on the role of mentoring as an act of martyrdom. Although it requires them to give up some of their time to be involved in the kinds of activities outlined earlier in this chapter, they will hopefully also benefit from the experience. Most mentors find that in order to explain their practice to a trainee, they need to re-evaluate it. This encourages them to engage in critical reflection too. An effective teacher will never stop analysing their practice and attempting to improve aspects of it no matter how long they have been teaching. The nature of the teaching profession means that you have never got it all sorted! It is a constant learning process. In recognition of this, the professional standards for post threshold teachers (i.e. those teachers breaking into the upper pay scale) specify that they should be able to act as role models for teaching and learning as well as providing regular coaching and mentoring for less experienced teachers. Mentoring trainees can therefore be used as evidence as part of a teacher's performance management, as well as encourage learning for its own sake as part of a teacher's continuing professional development (CPD). Hopefully then your mentor will benefit from and enjoy their role and be part of a learning team, along with you.

Summary

In this chapter I have outlined how SBT plays a key part in doing your PGCE at M-level. The role of critical reflection is essential in supporting you in your progress against the Professional Standards for QTS and enabling you to continue to develop throughout your career. Critical reflection enables you to understand the essential relationship between school-based and university-based elements of the PGCE, an element explored in the research–theory–practice model discussed in Chapter 1. The following key questions may help you to frame your thinking further:

- Do I know what critical reflection means and what a critically reflective teacher looks like?

- Do I know why critical reflection is important in order to develop professionally?

- Do I know how to go about developing the skills of critical reflection?

- Do I know how critically reflective skills may develop and progress during my SBT?

- Do I understand the role of my mentor in supporting me through this process?

 Further reading

Kyriacou, C. (2007) *Essential Teaching Skills*, 3rd edn. Cheltenham: Stanley Thornes. A key text for trainee teachers, exploring a range of aspects related to successful teaching and learning in both primary and secondary classrooms.

Loughran, J. (1996) *Developing Reflective Practice: Learning About Teaching and Learning Through Modelling*. London: Falmer Press. A very useful research-based book which explores the idea of reflective practice and impact on teaching and learning.

Tomlinson, P. (2007) *Understanding Mentoring: Reflective Strategies for School-Based Teacher Preparation*. Buckingham: Open University Press. A very useful reference for mentoring practice, providing insight into how to get the best out of your mentor–mentee relationship.

Wragg, E.C. (1999) *An Introduction to Classroom Observation*. London: RoutledgeFalmer. This book provides an insight into how teachers can identify and explore how their classrooms work using observation as a research method.

References

Fletcher, S. (2000) *Mentoring in Schools: A Handbook of Good Practice*. London: Kogan Page.

Furlong, J. and Maynard, T. (1995) *Mentoring Student Teachers*. London: Routledge.

Quality Assurance Agency (2001) *The Framework for Higher Education Qualifications in England, Wales and Northern Ireland*. Online at: http://www.qaa.ac.uk/academicinfrastructure/fheq/ewni/default.asp.

TDA (Training and Development Agency for Schools) (2007) *Professional Standards for Teachers*. London: TDA.

4 What is the relationship between research and development as a professional?

Tim Cain

As previous chapters have noted, the relationship between research, theory and practice in the developing professional is central to the PGCE M-level. This chapter aims to help you understand:

- the different types of research and the roles they play in professional development;

- the impact of research on the development of educational theories;

- the evolution of learning theory and its impact on practice;

- the range of approaches available to support research into your own practice;

- some of the ways in which you can avoid problems in your M-level research assignments.

What role does research play in my professional development?

Research is a means of acquiring knowledge. As humans, we seem to have a great need to know – people, places, facts and stories and so on – and we have invented lots of means to gain and record our knowledge. Our knowledge is hugely varied and obtained in many different ways: the way we get to know our friends is different from the way we learn that water boils at 100 degrees

Celsius. Not all knowledge is equally valuable; knowing how to get to work in the morning is probably more valuable than knowing which song was number one in the British music charts at Christmas 1975. Neither is all knowledge equally true; we can 'know' things to be false: for many years, it was accepted that the earth is at the centre of the universe.

Part of the story of human progress has been a continuing search to discover knowledge which is both valuable and true, and research is part of this story. Of course, not all research leads to true and valuable knowledge; a lot of research findings are worthless and/or of dubious validity. Nor is research the only path to valuable and true knowledge; much of what we hold to be valuable and true for us comes from everyday, personal experiences. However, research is a more trustworthy route to true and valuable knowledge than other means, including learning from everyday experience (which is unique to the individual), learning from others (who might be wrong) or operating on gut instinct (which can change from one day to the next). The focus on 'true' leads researchers to explain exactly how they came to know: the research methods they employed, exactly what happened and how they discovered their findings. The focus on 'valuable' leads researchers to link together bits of knowledge into coherent structures which we call theories.

One educational theory is that of Jean Piaget (1896–1980). Over many years, Piaget did a series of observations and experiments into how children think. He discovered that when he poured identical quantities of water into two identical jars, children of all ages could agree that the amounts of water were the same. However, when he transferred the water from one jar into a differently shaped jar, only the older children believed that the quantities of water hadn't changed; younger children thought that there was more water in a jar which was taller or fatter. Drawing on this and other experiments, Piaget found that children's thought changes qualitatively as they get older. He knitted together the knowledge obtained from different experiments to develop a theory of how children's thinking develops. His theory described in detail four successive stages of thinking.

Piaget's theory of child development had a number of practical implications for teachers. Because he demonstrated that young children think through active discovery, he inspired teaching that was practical, with children actively exploring and experimenting and thus constructing their own knowledge. Because he demonstrated that children's thinking changes, he inspired teaching that was better adapted to the intellectual level of children. These influences are now such a taken for granted part of the educational landscape that we can forget that before Piaget teaching was often considered to be a matter of imparting facts and assuming that if learners didn't understand it was because they were inherently stupid.

Educational theory

Educational theory can be more or less well developed; there is a continuum. Some classroom practices are so habitual that they are almost atheoretical; if you ask teachers, 'Why do you do that?' they might answer, 'Because it works'. Other practices are informed by partly developed and semi-articulated 'personal' theories. High-level theories are fully articulated, well worked out, tested, published and shown to work in a variety of circumstances. We can't theorize about everything, but it is helpful to understand what theories are, and it is also helpful to build your own theories on the theories of others. The following sections present a basic introduction to some theories of learning.

We learn by transmission

The 'learning as transmission' theory suggests that teachers have knowledge which they transmit to their pupils by teaching techniques such as telling, showing or explaining. It isn't a worked-out theory; in fact, it's almost a non-theory, but it's probably the 'default' theory that most people outside education have. (I suspect that many politicians have this theory because they tend to assume that problems – such as antisocial behaviour – can be addressed by education, such as citizenship lessons.) The chief problem with this theory is that it only works for very simple learning. ('Reggae comes from Jamaica. Where does Reggae come from?' 'Jamaica.' 'Correct.') Most often, if a teacher tells a class some facts, very few children actually learn what they're meant to learn. This is because the 'learning as transmission' theory fails to take account of essential matters of motivation and how learners interpret events (like lessons) in different ways.

We learn by seeking out pleasure and avoiding pain

A theory which was particularly popular in the middle of the last century was that human beings were essentially sophisticated animals. This was associated with a theory that we learn when we are motivated to do so, by either rewards or punishments. Because we are 'hard-wired' to seek out rewards and avoid punishments, we will try to produce behaviours (such as providing correct answers to teachers' questions) if we can be fairly certain that good things (such as praise) will result. Similarly, we avoid producing behaviours which lead to pain or discomfort. This theory is used today, often linked particularly to behaviour management. Research shows that rewards are more successful than punishments, but both are effective if they are quick, consistent and meaningful for the individuals concerned. A key writer about this theory is B.F. Skinner (1904–90), who distinguished between 'intrinsic' and 'extrinsic' motivation, stressing the need for teachers to move towards intrinsic motivation wherever possible. While this theory is supported by research evidence, and is better worked out than the previous theory, it tends to work best with simple learning, such as not calling out. One problem is that teachers and pupils can have different views about what constitutes rewards and punishments. So, for example, teachers can think they are motivating pupils when they praise them but pupils (perhaps responding to peer pressure) can view such praise as demotivating.

Learning is a natural human activity

A theory which has been popular since at least the time of Jean-Jacques Rousseau (1712–78) is that learning is natural and the job of the teacher is to provide environments which encourage it. The theory was given some impetus by Piaget and is also connected to the humanist, 'child-centred' philosophy advocated by Carl Rogers (1902–87) which suggests, among other things, that teachers should build their curriculum on the interests of their pupils. At the more extreme end of the theory, teachers should never do anything that might affect the free and natural development of the learner – they should stay out of the way for fear of imposing their own ideas. However, as with all theories, there are various ways of understanding them and most teachers who subscribe to this theory would say that they teach in accordance with natural development: encouraging, but not forcing, learners to develop more quickly and more effectively than they would without help.

Learning is about improving the brain

Whereas the previous theory was inspired mainly by philosophy, particularly moral philosophy, the 'improving the brain' theory was inspired mainly by psychology. Research studies, often in laboratory-like settings, found that learners learn through a process which starts with perception and ends with storing the learning in the long-term memory. Such studies enabled the development of a theory which says that people have ways of making sense of their experiences, for instance by organizing them into frameworks called 'schemata'. In this theory, new learning is hooked into already existing schemata, and the better and more numerous the hooks, the more effective the learning will be. A particular strength of the theory is that it explains why something which has been learned can be forgotten. It stresses the need to break up learning into manageable chunks, and for reinforcing what has already been learned. This theory is constantly being modified as a result of new work on the brain. However, while it explains how learning happens in individuals (for instance, in laboratory conditions), the disadvantage is that it tends to ignore the social element of much learning.

Learning is a social activity

Whereas cognitive psychologists were mainly interested in understanding how individuals made sense of their world, social psychologists were more interested in studying how children learned with the help of a parent or teacher. A major figure was the Russian psychologist Lev Vygotsky (1896–1934). Accepting that there were some things the children already knew and other things they didn't, he found that between these was a 'zone of proximal development' – things they knew (or could do) with assistance. Jerome Bruner (born 1915) developed this work, analysing ways in which teachers could 'scaffold' learning. The theory of learning as a social activity has since been extended to all aspects of learning. Thus this theory says that all learning, from the most important details down to how to behave in a playground, is constructed in association with others.

How can you relate to theories?

These thumbnail sketches are only a brief introduction to some educational theories; the first thing you should do is to try to understand them better. Do some reading, do some thinking and see if you can identify (a) which theories you believe most and (b) which theories are believed most by those around you, particularly your mentors. As you do so, you will come to realize (if you haven't already) that these are 'grand' theories, that is they operate at a high level of generalization and abstraction. To be a reflective teacher you will need more theories at lower levels – theories which help you decide what to teach next, how to answer pupils' questions and how best to structure your teaching. In particular, you'll want to engage with subject-specific theories about, for instance, how to teach poetry, or probability, or the science of sound.

 Activity

Consider your own learning. Under the headings used in this section, identify what you have learned using each of the theories explored. Are there things that you have learned which are more 'valuable' than others? In what ways do you learn best? Do you learn differently in different subject areas? How does how you learn influence the ways in which you teach? How have learning theories affected the development of the curriculum you are required to teach your pupils?

Finally, you need to know how to judge the quality of a theory. In general, a theory is considered good if it is internally consistent (all the bits relate to each other and make sense), if it is consistent with phenomena ('the facts'), if it explains events (as distinct from just describing them) and if it can be used to predict likely outcomes. We all have theories – you can't cross the road without having some sort of theory as to why you're doing it – and most are not based on research. But the theories which are supported by sound, robust and carefully carried out research are better than most.

Reading research

Working at M-level will almost certainly require you to read research and a major problem is that there is so much of it! It might help to consider some of the different types of research you might encounter: philosophical writing, reviews of literature, reflective writing, action research and empirical research. Although there is considerable overlap between the types, their purposes are different. It is also worth mentioning 'professional' literature, which tells teachers (and student teachers) how they should teach. Although such literature is often informed by research, it is not generally considered to be research as such (see Chapter 5).

Philosophical writing considers educational matters from a philosophical standpoint, that is from careful and reasoned thinking. Educational philosophers build arguments saying, in effect, 'If x is true, then it follows that a and b must also be true,' or, 'If x is true, then it follows that y and z cannot be true.' Philosophers build upon each other's work, frequently going back as far as Plato or Aristotle, and are concerned with making their arguments internally coherent. A good introduction to this type of writing is Richard Pring's *Philosophy of Education* (2005).

Literature reviews also build arguments, but with a firmer basis upon published research evidence. Some reviews summarize what has been published in a particular field, partly in order to highlight unexplored areas; for example, there are published literature reviews 'mapping' music education research in the UK, Scandinavia, Hong Kong and South America. Other reviews have a stronger focus on using the research evidence to inform practice. A good example is *Should We Be Using Learning Styles?* by Coffield et al. (2004), in which the authors review the relevant studies and demonstrate that very few learning style theories are valid and reliable.

Reflective writing is a rather loosely applied term which describes writing which is essentially personal. Its authors relate their own experiences to their knowledge, beliefs and values, often moved by a desire to describe educational situations they find unjust or repressive. Although reflective writing is expected to build arguments logically and to draw on evidence, there are not the same expectations as with philosophical methods; rather, it reflects the passion and commitment of its author. A good example is Jonathan Kozol's *Savage Inequalities: Children in America's Schools* (1992).

Action research is similarly based on the knowledge, beliefs and values of the author. The process of action research is often described as cyclical: researchers encounter problematic situations and act thoughtfully to improve them. Evaluation of their actions leads to planning and implementing new actions, which are then evaluated. The whole cycle is informed by the desire to improve matters, so action research includes reflective writing. A good collection of reflective writing and action research is *Action Research for Inclusive Education* by Felicity Armstrong and Michele Moore (2005).

Empirical research is probably the most common form of published research, and you will almost certainly be expected to read empirical research reports on your course. Empirical researchers formulate a research question and use research methods, such as observation, surveys, interviews or experiments, in an attempt to answer their question. A good example is the work Mary Budd Rowe undertook in the 1970s, observing primary science lessons. She found that teachers, having asked a question of pupils, waited for an average of only one second for a response. After listening to the pupils' responses, they waited an average of less than a second before they spoke again. However, when the two 'wait times' were increased to between three and five seconds, the pupils' responses were longer, more detailed and more thoughtful (Rowe, 1986).

Although various types of research writing exist in isolation, much educational research includes elements of several types. A common approach is for authors to begin by stating briefly why the focus of their research is important; this often requires reflective writing. Next, they review the literature around their focus, to show what is already known and to identify the gap that their own work attempts to fill. They then describe their empirical work, analyse their findings and present their conclusions. Finally, they will draw out the implications for practice: the action that future researchers (or action researchers) might take.

 Activity

Choose one journal article which describes research in your area of interest/expertise. Read it carefully and then consider the following questions:

- What was the point of the research? Why was it done?
- What happened? How was it conducted?
- What was discovered?
- How do these discoveries relate to the development of theory?
- Why should we believe the findings? How trustworthy are they?
- Overall, how good is the research?
- If the research is good, how might I use the findings?

Try to think about the impact such research could have on your own practice. Consider also what further questions reading the research raises and how you might go about finding answers to these.

Why should I research my own practice?

Sometimes, as beginning teachers, we can get a sense that everyone else knows better than we do, that we have little to add to the teaching profession and that we are entering a world in which all the answers are known: far from it. The nature of education means it is continually evolving, not just as a result of government changes and initiatives but because education is culturally and sociologically driven and the ways in which children respond or engage is not constant (even on an hour-by-hour basis in some cases!).

In Chapter 1 we discussed the notion of the 'visionary teacher' and the relationship between theory, research and practice in the developing professional, the key issue being that we cannot continue to use approaches just because they have worked well in the past or even because they work well now. Research enables us to explore why an approach works (or doesn't), it provides a platform for change, a basis for reflection and review, an opportunity to seek alternatives; it means that even those just entering the profession can make valuable contributions to the ways in which we educate children and young people.

A good starting point is always to think about learning. Consider the following in relation to your own practice:

- What learning takes place in your classroom and how do you know? Consider this at class, group and individual level. What qualitative and quantitative data do you have which will support your thinking? What does this data tell you? Which individuals or groups are performing particularly well/badly? Which ones are achieving around the level expected for their age yet are making little further progress?

- What affects learning in your classroom? Consider your teaching approaches, pupil's learning styles, length of lessons, the ways in which pupils are grouped/organized, the ethos within the classroom, pupil attitudes to learning, teacher attitudes to learning, pace of teaching, misconceptions, pupil engagement and motivation, teacher engagement and motivation, etc.

- What data would enable you to explore the issue(s) you identify further? For example, if you want to know what pupils think then how could you find this out? If you want to know whether grouping children differently impacts on learning what could you do?

- What methods could you use to collect data? Do you want to gather quantitative or qualitative data? What could you read to enable you to make your decision and design your research?

- What ethical issues are involved in carrying out your research? Do you need to seek anyone's permission? Is your research of a sensitive nature? Is your approach fair to all pupils or does it benefit one group more than another?

- How could you compare your findings with those of others to identify similarities and differences? What could account for these differences – choice of methodology, context of school, type of sample? How significant are these differences and do they point to a possible evolution in teaching and learning?

- What impact does your research have on your own practice? Is there scope for change and how will you monitor and evaluate this? Is there value in communicating your research more widely? What ethical issues may be raised in involving a wider audience?

The answers to these questions will be highly personal and context-driven and, as a result, it is difficult to prescribe a common approach which will serve all educational research. However, the following section provides an insight into the approaches you could use, exploring these through case studies.

How do I research my own practice?

Different courses vary in the types of research they expect their M-level students to undertake. Some insist on empirical work and others expect only literature reviews, reflective or philosophical writing; it is important to be clear about your own institution's stance. Whatever is expected of you, the essential starting point is to find a suitable focus, preferably arising from your experience in school. The following cases might give you some ideas.

 Philosophical writing

In his French lessons Rajesh found that he was required to give regular pencil and paper tests to his pupils. Because the school was selective, many of the pupils scored high marks, but Rajesh was sure that the tests, which required mostly one-word answers, were not adequate for assessing deeper understandings and actually helped to convince the pupils that simple recall was more important than having to think. Using Dewey's writing about reflection he wrote a philosophical essay, asking, 'What are the necessary and sufficient conditions for us to say that children have correctly learned new French vocabulary?'

Literature reviews

Jane had previously worked as a teaching assistant, having had responsibility for a five-year-old with ADHD. She had already read something about ADHD and had experienced considerable success with her five-year-old. When she was told that her class of 10- and 11-year-olds included eight children with ADHD she was not overly concerned, but when she was told that they had all been prescribed Ritalin she was horrified. She was certain that most ADHD children's behaviour could be managed without medication and set out to provide evidence, from the medical and educational literature, for her case. She didn't succeed as she had hoped because she found conflicting evidence. However, her work, in terms of the range of the literature she consulted and the depth of analysis, was considered to be a good example of M-level work.

 ## Reflective writing

Tony's placement was in a boys' secondary school. During their lunch break the boys were required to be outside; the doors were closed and dinner supervisors were employed to ensure that only boys with legitimate reasons for being in the building entered. Talking to some of his tutor group, Tony realized that the prevailing practice of playing large, aggressive games of football in the playground made it difficult for those who disliked football. He was reminded of his own school days, when he had stood on the margins of the playground, feeling physically and psychologically excluded because he disliked football himself. He arranged, through his mentor, to start a chess club (a legitimate lunchtime activity!) for some of his tutor group, and he kept a diary of its activities. His writing included quotes from his diary, including a wry account of his conversation with a dinner supervisor who objected to the fact that there were far more boys in the club than could be accommodated on his chess sets!

 ## Action research

Charlotte wanted to research the endings of her class music lessons: the 'final plenary' or summing up. With permission from her mentor, she audio-recorded the last ten minutes of three lessons. At the same time she read about the plenary and discovered that she had only a rough idea of its purpose; she hadn't realized that it is intended for the pupils to reflect on their own learning processes. Listening to her recordings she understood that her final plenaries were dominated by her – she spoke for over 80 per cent of the time and expected clear, 'correct' answers to her questions. This approach, she wrote, was 'contravening the purpose of the plenary!' She put in place an action plan for improving her final plenaries, recorded five more lessons and analysed the improvements in her teaching.

Empirical research

Sanja was motivated by the large number of overweight pupils in her secondary school. Her literature review showed that pupils should have sustained periods of aerobic exercise three or more times per week, but she knew that many pupils were excused from their PE lessons and she suspected that many parents were unaware of the importance of physical exercise. Originally she planned to interview parents of overweight children but her mentor pointed out that there were considerable ethical difficulties involved. She ended up interviewing all the pupils in her class, asking them what physical activities they did, how often and the reasons for them undertaking these activities. Drawing on her own observation, she compared the interviews with the five pupils she thought were the most overweight with those of the five she considered to be the least overweight. She found that some pupils in both groups had less than an hour's physical activity per week, but could not show a significant correlation between the amount of physical activity they did and their weight. She concluded that the causes of the pupils' being overweight were more complex than the amount of physical activity they did and that a thorough approach to health education should not focus exclusively on physical exercise.

Research and professional development

The cases described above did not exactly discover new facts about education, nor did they generate new educational theories. However, the students who wrote them engaged with literature to explore and understand questions they believed important. This involved them responding to what they read, agreeing and disagreeing, thinking through contradictions and generating ideas of their own. They related all of this to their own practice as developing teachers within their placement schools. Doubtless they wrote because they were required to but, as a reader and marker, I felt that they wrote as a way of ordering their own values, beliefs, thoughts and feelings into a coherent, and sometimes passionate, piece of writing. The processes involved – reading, researching, thinking, writing, editing and rewriting – developed them as people and as teachers. Their reflection on the topics they researched became truly well informed. If you approach research assignments with an open mind, a thirst to know more, a belief in the importance of thinking things through and a passion for teaching, you might find that your assignment stops being just a chore and becomes a means of developing your values, beliefs, thoughts and feelings in a way that affects the way you are, in school.

Formulating a research question

Researching your own practice is an integral part of studying the PGCE at M-level. Research into your own teaching enables you to explore complex issues, problems or strategies, such as how to manage behavioural problems, how to explain difficult concepts, how to relate to parents or teaching assistants, how to ask questions and respond to pupils' answers. In these cases, research questions could be constructed such as: 'How do I . . . (manage behaviour, involve TAs, or use questioning)?' 'How might I do this better?' In attempting to answer such questions you will draw on both professional literature and research literature to articulate the ways in which you would like to develop your own professional practice. PGCE trainees under my supervision have researched a broad range of areas, investigating their own teaching and issues such as student voice, KS2–3 transition, out-of-school learning and emotional literacy. In so doing, they have formulated research questions such as the following:

Teaching: What do students learn when I teach them . . . (to write persuasively/about the states of matter/about the Tudors, etc.)? What do students like and dislike about my teaching? How can I improve my use of whole-class discussions?

Student voice: To what extent are pupils' opinions considered in the running of schools? To what extent do individual teachers ask pupils to evaluate their lessons? How good are school councils as a means of teaching democratic values?

KS2–3 transition: What pupil records are transferred from primary to secondary school and how are these used? What are Year 6 pupils' hopes and fears about their move to secondary school, and to what extent are these realized? What arrangements does a secondary school make to help new pupils to settle into school and how do pupils respond to these arrangements?

Out-of-school education: What do teachers perceive to be the educational benefits of a school trip, and how does this compare with the pupils' perceptions? How does a visit to an art gallery develop pupils' understanding of visual art? How do teachers view the benefits and risks of taking pupils out of school?

Emotional literacy: How can drama be used to teach pupils to be more emotionally literate, and how can improvements in emotional literacy be assessed? How are pupils taught to manage their anger, and which means are most effective in the case of three individual pupils? How does the school counsellor perceive her role, and how does this compare with teachers' perceptions?

While some have chosen to answer such questions drawing purely on their own thoughts and their own reading, many have chosen to use some empirical research methods, including questionnaires, interviews, observations and data analysis. It is probably worth considering, at this point, what methods you would use to answer each of the above research questions. Which questions would involve seeking the views of teachers? pupils? parents or others?

Reflective Activity

Audio tape yourself teaching a lesson. Choose three five-minute periods (perhaps one towards the beginning, one in the middle and one towards the end) and identify how many and what types of questions are asked by you and by your pupils. Which pupils answer the questions. Now time the period between you asking a question and following up: the 'wait time'. How long do you wait for children to respond? We are going to use this information to develop your questioning skills.

First read the article by Mary Budd Rowe (1986) 'Wait time: slowing down may be a way of speeding up' to see how your times compare with the findings from other research. It is very likely that your wait time is similar to that found in other classrooms.

Identify three strategies you could use to increase your wait time and practise these for the next two weeks. Audio tape a lesson again and see if there were any changes. If not, start again with developing and practising your strategies. If there were changes, move on to the next stage of development.

Analyse the questions asked by yourself and your pupils. What is the purpose of these questions? What responses do they elicit and from whom? Are there particular questions which promote learning? Who controls this dialogue? Identify three things which you would like to develop in terms of questioning in the classroom and develop strategies to achieve these. For example, if your pupils lack the confidence to ask more questions verbally, you could use a questions box in the classroom for children to write them down.

Sometimes working on wait time can increase pupil–pupil dialogue in the classroom so you may find that the first stage of this activity does impact on the second stage.

Research methods

If you had unlimited resources at your disposal you might have a wide choice as to which research methods you would use. Because you are likely to be undertaking your research at the same time as learning to teach (and doing both within a short time span) your choices will be limited, but this doesn't mean that you need to produce research of poor quality. For example, although you might prefer to survey a representative sample of 1,000 pupils, you might need to survey an unrepresentative 30. However, there are benefits to be had if you are familiar with these particular pupils; if you use what you know of the pupils and design a questionnaire which both gets to the heart of what you want to know and is absolutely on their wavelength, you might have more reliable findings than if you survey a greater number whom you don't know. Similarly, if you want to enquire as to whether pupils' SATs results at Year 9 are reliable indicators of their

GCSE results, you might prefer to sample the results across the whole country, but locating the study in your placement school might lead to findings which are taken more seriously within this school than a nationwide survey!

Having formulated your research question and methods, there are many texts which tell you how to carry out educational research. Many people find Judith Bell's *Doing Your Research Project* (2005) a useful starting point for empirical work, while a more in-depth understanding can be provided by a careful reading of *Research Methods in Education* by Cohen et al. (now in its sixth edition (2007)) or *Real World Research* by Colin Robson (2002). Jean McNiff's *Action Research for Professional Development* (2002) is a helpful guide to action research, and has the advantage of being published online. *Reflective Practice* by Gillie Bolton is a helpful text for stimulating reflective or philosophical writing. There are also specific texts about aspects of research such as designing questionnaires, analysing documents, carrying out interviews and statistical analysis. In my view, it is best to decide what method to use, and to focus your reading on this method; try not to get too bogged down. Occasionally you should stop reading and ask yourself questions such as:

- What exactly is my research question?

- Why is this question interesting or important?

- Is it likely that my research methods will answer this question?

- What might I discover?

- How might my tutors criticize my research?

- How might I respond to criticism?

You should make every attempt to strengthen your research so that it is difficult for a reader to argue that you have invented your findings or imposed your own views on the evidence. However, no research is perfect, and it is quite helpful to acknowledge the limitations of your research, so long as these are not too great!

Ethics

As soon as you start to use research methods you inevitably find yourself facing ethical dilemmas. In Sanja's case (see above) it would clearly have been insulting to tell a parent 'I am interested in researching your views about physical activity, because you are the parent of an overweight child.' Sanja might have been tempted to solve this problem by not divulging the full purpose of her research, by saying, 'I am interested in researching parents' views about physical activity.' Such an evasive approach might not be given ethical approval, on the grounds that if the purpose of the research became public (as research should be, if it is to count as research) the parent might read it and feel that she had misled them. Neither was it ethical for Sanja to interview pupils without telling them the purpose of the research. However, telling them that she would compare the most and the least overweight would run the risk of causing them hurt. Thus Sanja had to find an ethical balance between telling them openly what she would do with her interview data and not causing hurt. She was reasonably open with them about the purposes of her research. She explained how their anonymity would be maintained in the research report and gave them the right to 'opt out' of the research without any penalties. She also understood the need to consult, through her mentor, the school managers. As it happened, they did not require her to request permission from the pupils' parents or guardians, but in another school this might have been necessary.

Charlotte (see above) had fewer ethical issues because she was researching her own practice. Nevertheless, it was still necessary for her to tell the pupils why their lessons were being recorded and to give them an opportunity to opt out. She had to assure them that they would be anonymized and that her recording would not be used for any purpose other than her research. (If any of them had objected, she would have needed to discuss, with her mentor, how best to respond.) Matters of ethics, which are essentially to do with respecting people's rights, have become steadily more important in recent years, and are likely to become more so. If the research is good, it might tell people something they don't already know, and this can be hurtful. There are very few rules that can be straightforwardly applied in all circumstances, so what supervisors and ethical committees do is to ask questions such as: 'In what ways, and to what extent, might people's rights be infringed by this research?' 'Is the knowledge that might be generated by this research worth a small infringement of rights?' 'Might the research question be answered with less infringement of people's rights?' If you are considering action research or empirical research you need to consider such questions before you carry out the research, and to write about your ethical approach in your assignment.

Data collection

Keep your data manageable and simple. Obviously you need your data to be sufficient to answer your research question but you don't want too much! On our course, we would be happy with questionnaire surveys of 30 pupils, four or five focus group interviews or six to eight individual interviews. Literature reviews can be limited to 15–20 academic articles – fewer if the review is part of an empirical study. We consider the issue of quantity as less important than quality. (Although your tutors should be able to provide a rough guide as to what is acceptable, they might not be very precise for the same reason.) As any good research methods text will tell you, it's helpful once you've drawn up your questionnaire or interview schedule to trial it with one or two people – you may be surprised at how often questions which make perfect sense to you are misunderstood by others. It's also worth considering whether you could adopt a reasonably imaginative approach to data collection. For instance, if you want to research pupils' views, might you ask them to draw something, prior to talking to you? Might it be helpful to show them images and ask them to talk about them?

Data analysis

Before you collect data, you need to have a reasonably clear idea of how you will analyse them. Will your data be quantitative, consisting of numbers, or qualitative, consisting of words? If numbers, do you have a sufficient grasp of statistics to understand the significance of your figures? Do you understand how to use SPSS or similar software? If words, will you apply predetermined categories of analysis or will you let these emerge from the data? Data analysis is the core of research; you should aim to do high-quality analysis of small amounts of data, rather than the opposite. Again, research methods texts can help you get to grips with data analysis but can also be off-putting if you concentrate too much on the theory; it's better to get started on your analysis, even if you make mistakes the first time around.

Sanja and Charlotte used both quantitative and qualitative methods. Sanja calculated the average number of hours per person spent on physical activities undertaken by the whole class, by the most overweight and by the least overweight, and she compared these. She also analysed qualitative data about reasons for different physical activities, with categories including social benefits, enjoyment and achievement. Charlotte transcribed her final plenaries and compared the number of words spoken by her with the number spoken by pupils. She categorized the nature of the pupils' participation as 'group discussion', 'class discussion', 'questioning' and 'performing'. Using both qualitative and quantitative data helped these students to undertake a more detailed analysis than relying on only one type of data; depending on your research question, it can result in higher quality research.

Development of theory

Connecting your own research with the 'bigger picture' will help you develop theoretical understandings. In Sanja's case, she wrote a review of literature around health education: what it means, what is known about it and why it is important. In Charlotte's case, she analysed what had been written about plenaries – why they are considered important, why whole-class learning benefits individuals and how plenaries can aid metacognition. Having written their literature reviews, both students were able to connect their own findings to what they had read, articulating theories about the necessity for health education to be focused on a variety of factors including exercise (Sanja) and the challenges of implementing effective plenaries (Charlotte). These theories led them to consider how other teachers might use their research findings (i.e. implications for practice) and what other research might follow (implications for research).

Problems with M-level research assignments

Although the majority of assignments students produce are of an appropriate quality for M-level, some fall short of the expected standard and certain problems occur quite frequently. First, some students spend an inordinate amount of their assignments describing the background to their study – their school, its systems, its staff and pupils. Almost always, the criteria for M-level include the necessity to be analytical rather than descriptive. This doesn't mean that you cannot describe what is relevant, but it does mean that pure description should be kept to a minimum. If you find you have written more than 300 words about your school, it's worth asking yourself if it is all really relevant.

A similar problem exists in reflective writing. Heartfelt descriptions are interesting ('This is what I experienced, this is what I felt') but they need to be integrated with answers to questions beginning with 'Why'. There is a difference between writing about your values, beliefs, thoughts and feelings in an academic assignment and simply emoting, as you might do in a blog. In both Jane's and Tony's assignments (see earlier) they had to consider reasons for the practice: why Ritalin was so widely prescribed (Jane) and why pupils were required to be outside (Tony). Because Tony was writing a reflective piece, he had to consider why he responded as he did to this requirement and why others might respond differently. Jane also touched on these matters, but because hers was a literature review she focused much more on what others had written.

A third problem occurs when there is insufficient focus to the assignment. Students can spend hours designing nicely produced, pupil-friendly questionnaires which, when completed, are analysed by means of colourful graphs and pie charts, but don't actually answer the research questions. I remember one assignment which asked pupils a number of questions about their journeys to school – how far they travelled, whether they came by car, bus or walked, what time they arrived at school and so on. The problem was that the research question was, 'Why do Year 7 pupils choose to attend school X?' This question was clear and researchable. It had the possibility to link with more important questions, such as whether pupils or their parents determine which secondary school is attended. It even had potential to inform the school's marketing policy. The problem was that the student had already decided the answer – he thought that pupils attended school X because it was convenient for travelling. He was unable to connect his research to the research question and his assignment ended up disjointed and confused (although immaculately presented).

What have assignments to do with my professional development?

Whether you produce excellent M-level assignments or just scrape by, the process of writing the assignments should aid your professional development. On completion, you should feel that you have examined one question critically and in some depth. Even if your work is dissatisfying for you, you will have had to answer educational questions such as: 'How do I know that this is true?' 'What is the evidence?' 'Does it stack up?' Although clearly you will have addressed such questions before, it is important to ask them of educational practices, particularly teaching and learning. Learning to teach is practical, and the craft of teaching can sometimes appear to be disconnected from the theory, but all teachers have some theories and good teachers have good theories. Research assignments are intended to help you develop your own theories and, more importantly, to develop a habit of theorizing so that you can put into practice the relationship between theory, research and practice once you have your own class. Chapter 5 will provide further support on how to put down your ideas in writing.

Summary

This chapter has shown that research offers us a valuable means of analysing and evaluating both our own practice and wider educational issues. It enables us to explore complex concepts and to develop our own practice to meet the needs of pupils in the future. It is this which ensures that education continues to move forward and respond to change. Think of your own schooling. What things have changed since you left school and why do you think this is? What do you think will be the 'big issues' for the future in education? How do you think your own research can contribute to the body of knowledge which already exists in this area?

Further reading

Burnaford, G., Fischer, J. and Hobson, D. (2000) *Teachers Doing Research: The Power of Action Through Inquiry*, 2nd edn. Abingdon: Routledge. Provides some really useful examples of action research in practice and puts teachers at the heart of change in their classrooms.

Pritchard, A. and Woollard, J. (2010) *Psychology for the Classroom: Constructivism and Social Learning*. Oxford: Routledge/David Fulton Education. Provides useful insight into some of the debates around interactivity and constructivist learning in the classroom.

Wilson, E. (ed.) (2009) *School-Based Research: A Guide for Education Students*. London: Sage. A very supportive read for those developing classroom-based research, taking those new to this field through the process from research design to analysis and presentation of data.

Woollard, J. (2010) *Psychology for the Classroom: Behaviourism*. Oxford: Routledge/David Fulton Education. A thought-provoking read into the ways in which behaviourism underpins learning and behaviour management in the classroom.

References

Armstrong, F. and Moore, M. (2005) *Action Research for Inclusive Education: Changing Places, Changing Practices, Changing Minds*. Abingdon: RoutledgeFalmer.

Bell, J. (2005) *Doing Your Research Project: A Guide for First-Time Researchers in Education, Health and Social Science*, 4th edn. Maidenhead: Open University Press.

Bolton, G. (2005) *Reflective Practice: Writing and Professional Development*, 2nd edn. London: Sage.

Coffield, F., Moseley, D., Hall, E. and Ecclestone, K. (2004) *Should We Be Using Learning Styles? What Research Has to Say to Practice*. London: Learning and Skills Research Centre, LSDA. Online at: http:// www.lsda.org.uk/pubs/dbaseout/download.asp?code=1543.

Cohen, L., Manion, L. and Morrison, K. (2007) *Research Methods in Education*, 6th edn. London: RoutledgeFalmer.

Kozol, J. (1992) *Savage Inequalities: Children in America's Schools*. New York: HarperCollins.

McNiff, J. (2002) *Action Research for Professional Development: Concise Advice for New Action Researchers*, 3rd edn. Online at: http://www.jeanmcniff.com/booklet1.html.

Pring, R. (2005) *Philosophy of Education: Aims, Theory, Common Sense and Research*. London: Continuum.

Robson, C. (2002) *Real World Research: A Resource for Social Scientists and Practitioner-researchers*. Oxford: Blackwell.

Rowe, M.B. (1986) 'Wait time: slowing down may be a way of speeding up!', *Journal of Teacher Education*, 37 (1): 43–50.

5 How does academic writing at M-level make me a better teacher?

Kate Domaille

Often students find it difficult to understand why they should be writing academic essays on a course which leads to a professional qualification. As explained in Chapter 1, the PGCE M-level requires the synthesis of theory, research and practice which, in turn, supports both academic and professional development. This chapter will help you make the transition from level 6 to level 7 through:

- establishing the difference between the two levels of academic writing;

- identifying ways in which you can develop as a critical reader and writer;

- supporting you in using literature sources more effectively;

- considering the expectations of your tutors and interpreting their feedback on your work;

- reflecting on the relationship between academia and professional practice.

Behind many university providers' decision to award Masters level credits with the PGCE was the notion that a good practitioner of teaching is an enquiring one, exploring professional issues and concerns with an open mind and an eye to solving their own problems in the workplace. The university-based and school-based elements of the PGCE M-level are not exclusive but rather interact, enabling and supporting the reflective phases described by the model in Chapter 3. In Chapter 1, the notion that the PGCE M-level is harder than the PGCE H-level was hopefully refuted and I intend to contribute to this stance by arguing that developing one's research interests alongside professional demands need not be an overload of responsibility. In fact I will argue that research supports your role as a classroom practitioner, informing how you can further question and resolve your own classroom difficulties. Writing about that understanding in a formal way, to achieve Masters-level credits, is the element of additional work that cannot be underestimated. Nevertheless, work taken at a high level of reflection and analysis is likely to inform your practice at a deep and enduring level.

What is my tutor looking for in my academic study?

University PGCE tutors have professional backgrounds as teachers. Their interest is in schools, in teaching and learning, in assessment, in pupils, in curriculum and in policy. So, while some of them may occasionally appear a bit remote in their own studies, they usually have a good understanding of the myriad of difficulties attending to working in a school environment.

There will inevitably be variations in tutor expectations of trainees' work at Masters level according to the research traditions evident in different sectors of education (primary or secondary schools) and in different methodological preferences (quantitative or qualitative enquiries), as well as different university expectations of what the Masters-level credits are awarded for. Most universities will opt for extended essay submissions in the region of 5,000–6,000 words, but you should expect that each university will have different ways of organizing the assessment. One element of an M-level submission, for example, could be for students to give a conference-style presentation on their research, receiving feedback on their ideas – in addition to the writing. Despite the obvious variances, there will be one unifying expectation tutors will have of you and that is that you are interested in knowing more. Your own practice will reveal early on that the problems teachers face are manifold and complex. There really are no easy solutions.

Learning *how* to teach is bound to occupy most of your time in the initial stages of your training, but this will quickly become subordinate to the consideration of how to teach more effectively. Efficient lessons can be prepared but effective lessons require more understanding. This latter issue – becoming more effective – is one that should drive your studies forward in the PGCE year and inform how you view the relationship between theory and practice in your PGCE M-level year.

From H-level to M-level

PGCE courses have a long history of a variety of assessment procedures. A great deal of value has always been placed on written reflections, critical analysis of classrooms and how they work, understanding of policy and curriculum development, and understanding of teaching and learning styles. Even when your course has an M-level award attached to it, all of the above expectations for knowing how schools work are likely to remain: indeed they are vital to demonstrate competence against the Professional Standards for QTS. For example, the Professional Standards which require trainees to have knowledge and understanding of a range of teaching, learning and behaviour management strategies and to know how to use and adapt them could be evidenced in all kinds of ways at a practical level. You could:

- attend lectures and make notes;

- attend seminars and workshops where you can put some of the ideas into practice;

- read the documentation on various teaching, learning and behaviour management strategies independently;

- observe and evaluate how teachers use and apply these strategies in school;

- experiment in your own practice, then have it observed and advised upon.

All of these activities, and more besides, are evidence of standard H-level skills and expectations, working literally at a higher level by having to *know*, *understand* and *use* them.

In training, a balance has to be struck between 'showing' and 'telling' you how it works (lectures and seminars) and you learning through 'doing', through the teaching. All teachers are involved in continuing professional development in schools, although as delivered by schools this tends to be focused around how new initiatives and ideas will be implemented. Once teachers become more confident and assured in their role in school it is common for them to undertake further education. Teachers wishing to increase subject knowledge, or develop expertise in a specific area, for example Special Educational Needs, or develop their skills as managers, all undertake further study. Being involved in solving educational problems is a professional responsibility and it can be managed through wider reading and in-depth study. The Masters component of the PGCE is a good way to begin that further training.

While experience tells us that the two roles of training for the profession and for the academic award can work together, the situation is not without some tension. Some trainees and teachers in schools worry that if universities begin to involve PGCE trainees in Masters research they may be distracting them from practical understanding. Most universities have not simply swapped one kind of training with another, that is replaced practice-based knowledge with research knowledge, but rather have moved to develop research knowledge out of the practice. This is an assertion I want to elaborate on in this chapter; theory doesn't detract from practice, but enhances and improves it. Additionally, managing competing priorities and expectations is one of the extraordinary skills teachers need to excel in! In the case studies below you will see that theory and practice can indeed be happy bedfellows, each informing the other.

Look back at the professional standards relating to teaching, learning and behaviour management and consider these in relation to Karen.

Case study: Karen

Karen is an English teacher on her teaching practice in an inner-city secondary school. She has noticed that the boys in her lower set Year 8 group are very disaffected. They fidget, swing on their chairs, disrupt the class and shout out. Their behaviour is never good but is particularly pronounced whenever they are asked to settle to the task of writing. Sometimes she has found ways to manage their behaviour but the writing is never completed. It is really bothering her.

At a *professional* level Karen has a number of options open to her:

- She can discuss her problems with the class teacher.

- She can discuss the problems more widely in the school.

- She can develop her knowledge and understanding further of a range of teaching, learning and behaviour management strategies.

- She might observe another teacher taking the class looking for hints and clues as to how to engage the boys.

- She can be observed, asking for feedback on her approaches and strategies.

- She can shadow the class for a day to witness any noticeable change in attitude and learning across the curriculum.

- She can continue to adapt her teaching.

All the above strategies and targets for improving the situation are valid, and indeed a good school mentor would advise these and more to try to unpick the problem. Karen knows she has made progress with the behaviour but she cannot understand what the issues are with the writing. She wants to know what it is about writing that they find so difficult. What wider questions does this scenario raise?

Key questions would include:

- Is this a problem because she is a trainee teacher and lacks experience? (It is tempting to start from this point but it's not always the answer.)

- Is this just boys being boys?

- Is this a problem with *what* she is teaching them or *how* she is teaching them?

- Is it just Karen's problem or is she experiencing an issue that is felt more widely in (a) the school? (b) the local area? (c) nationally?

- Are there ways to solve the problem?

- Are there any clues in the theory?

Karen has identified a number of lines of enquiry by exploring in her initial questions where the problem lies. It may be that in formalizing some of these questions she might be able to begin to identify ways forward. To refine her research further Karen needs to follow a clear plan of action.

Figure 5.1 illustrates how Karen has identified practical questions to drive her study. The academic enquiry will support her understanding further. She can combine her practical needs with academic ones. Some of the answers to her problems can be discovered by collecting data in school and asking members of staff. This will enable her to view the specific problems of one class within the context of her school. This is a good starting point and may help her to begin to untangle the very self-critical stance she began with, that it was her 'beginner' status that was the issue. Through investigating the problem more extensively she might shift her viewpoint from seeing it as entirely one she is experiencing alone, to a problem that is representative of wider concerns in the teaching of writing. It should empower her because if she maintains the position that her inexperience is the overriding cause of the problem, she will not be able to enact any real change to that problem. Knowing more about the problem challenges the view that inexperience is a barrier. She can overcome inexperience through gaining wider knowledge.

Figure 5.1 shows how the enquiry can move from practice to theory and back again. Informally Karen has deployed a number of different methods to find things out. She has decided to:

- *collect observations* of herself teaching;

- *undertake observations* of others teaching the same group;

- *ask the school for data* on boys' achievement;

- *ask the head of department* or other teachers for their perspectives on the problem.

The initial lines of enquiry will have answered some questions and thrown up new ones. Each line of enquiry should enable a student to adjust the question and refine what they want to know. The main development in the research would be to begin to see the issue under analysis as a 'case study' of something more wide-reaching. Once this stage is reached the problems are no longer so individualized to you and your classroom but part of a professional exchange of ideas about how all teachers try to manage educational issues. Now the more formal process can begin.

And so to reading . . .

All PGCE students need to learn to read strategically from the vast amount of literature on offer. Some guidance on assessing your abilities to do that are given later in the chapter, in Table 5.1.

Some educational issues are very well researched. Karen's case study on boys has been

Investigate professionally first

And then academically

Individual: Is the problem because I am a trainee teacher? *Ask* for observations on yourself with your interactions with boys the focus – use observations on others to explore relationship between teacher and boys in the classroom.

Does experience matter? Do teacher approaches affect pupil performance? Start literature search: *Key words* – 'teacher attitudes' and 'boys'. What does the literature say about boy behaviour and teacher response?

School: Do all boys in this school underachieve compared to girls? *Find out* school data. Look at results data. Is this an issue the school is working on? *Ask* your head of department. *Ask* other teachers. Be careful here: teachers have different perspectives, not all of them are fact! *Look at professional literature* for overviews and insights, e.g. Ofsted reports.

What is being argued about boys and achievement? Why do boys seem to underachieve? Is it in English or more widespread? How does the literature discuss the role of schools in the achievement of boys? Is about curriculum? Resources? Teaching and learning methods? (*Search* 'Boys and English'; 'Boys and interactive learning'; 'Boys and motivation'; 'Boys and writing'.)

In the local area: Is my school different from or representative of the local population? What is the school population like? Does this matter? (See professional literature.) Is the local authority responding to the issue? *Ask* your mentor, head of department?

Is this local problem representative of a national problem? How does this class, this school, this area compare to the national statistics about boys?

Can investigate local information about schools performance and Ofsted reports about boys' attainment.

Are we talking all boys – or some boys? Are boys a single category? What's the difference between boys' achievement in different ethnic groups or from different social classes? What about high attaining boys?

What are the arguments being made about boys and learning?

Is it biological/cognitive – do boys learn differently?

Is sociological – do they prefer to learn more interactively?

Is it pedagogical – is the curriculum too 'feminine'?

Is it cultural – boys' roles and expectations are changing and girls are doing better?

What do I now know? And what can I do about it? If I've found out that what I am teaching them is unengaging, can I change it? Can I teach the same material but in a new way? Can I make adjustments and measure the differences? I can ask for new observations to be done on my teaching of this group and compare these to earlier ones to see if there are any significant differences.

Drawing conclusions: I've collected a lot of data – school data, observations, interview notes and conversations – and I have a good idea of the problem in school. I have explored what I have found out in relation to wider reading about boys and underachievement. I am beginning to believe that the problem isn't me but is the result of multiple factors, some personal, some cultural. It has made a difference to adjust my language in the classroom and my expectations. The problem hasn't gone but it is better managed.

Figure 5.1 Relationship between professional and academic questions

researched at length and from a variety of perspectives. Concern about boys' performance in schools is a regular feature of the news and most of the stakeholders in education have perspectives and opinions on it. Karen isn't going to have any trouble connecting with a corpus of research work on her issue. What she might have to take care with is how the issue is *debated*, *organized* and *written about* so she can get a sense of what the different paradigms are. She needs to find ways of climbing the mountain of literature. You can think of the literature in two broad categories.

Professional literature

Professional literature describes a large body of work usually issued by government agencies and subject associations or lobbying bodies. The quality of professional literature varies hugely. Some examples might be digests of academic literature and research studies (some Ofsted publications are a good example in this genre) and can provide a good overview of an area. Others offer soundbites or teaching advice and are meant to act as professional guidance. Professional literature can be a good starting point for getting the 'feel' of an area or an understanding of the debates associated with it but it is important to note that not all professional literature findings have been based on careful research.

Good sources of 'digests' of an educational issue are the websites related to government policy and publications. Since writing this chapter for the first edition in 2008, there has been a change of government and schools' organization and policies are under extensive review. Both the Department for Education and Ofsted are reasonable repositories of research digests and summaries of practical problems (http://www.education.gov.uk; http://www.ofsted.gov.uk). It is also worth visiting your subject association website for guidance about current thinking and issues within your subject area.

Academic literature

Academic literature is distinguished from professional literature in being based on research. This will again be varied in 'feel'. Some articles, chapters and books are based on theoretical analyses of particular educational phenomena, applying theoretical models about pedagogy and practice to specific incidences, while others detail the outcomes of carefully constructed classroom studies of teacher performance or pupil performance. Some will show tables of findings or other research data. But not all educational research is based on classroom research. A lot of academic chapters and articles look at educational policy or curriculum.

As a teacher operating under specific frameworks and expectations, the role of professional literature is important. It advises and shapes what happens in the classroom. Academic literature might be argued to question some of the assumptions that may be evident in professional literature, using data to inform whether or if certain approaches, initiatives or guidance retain value.

Activity

Some of you will be new graduates and have the process of study fresh in your minds. Others will have been out of formal study for some time so some of the processes of reading and writing critically may be daunting initially. Let us start by considering how to read critically.

Try the self-assessment test in Table 5.1. Suggestions are given for targets to improve.

Table 5.1 Being a critical reader

Criteria The critical reader is able to:	Self-assessment rating: 1 = excellent; 2 = good; 3 = emerging skills; 4 = skills yet to be acquired	Targets and date
Recognize how the text is organized (role of abstracts, titles, headings and sub-headings)		Skim and scan two searched articles using the organizational features to suggest whether the article is worth reading.
Select central themes		After reading try to identify key points.
Select subsidiary/associated information		
Distinguish different kinds of reasoning used		
Select evidence required for task		When reading, if something interesting grabs your attention, highlight it or mark it gently with pencil. It could be a quote for later.
Understand subject-specific terminology		Make a list of words you want clarified – e.g. paradigm, taxonomy, pedagogy.
Identify theoretical underpinning of the information		Has the writer based the article on specific research? Is it opinion-led?
Interpret research data		What do the graph, pie chart, quotes from interviews show?

Synthesize the key points of the information		Can you summarize the article quickly in two sentences?
Evaluate the information		Did it say something you are interested in even if you don't agree with it?
Search electronic sources for information		Contact the librarian, ask for help. Seek guidance from university tutors. Argue for information to be included in guidance handouts.

Using the library

PGCE trainees are frequently away from the university in schools. However, the digital age permits you wide access to academic literature through journals and databases accessible through the web. Being registered at the university affords you access to electronic databases from home. Consult the library for this. Then, at the touch of a button, and a careful search through the library catalogue, it is possible to download journal articles to your desktop. Even at a distance you can be a researcher.

Karen decided to search the electronic databases using some key words and phrases gained from her trawl through the professional literature:

- Boys and English

- Boys and motivation

- Boys and writing

- Boys and interactive learning

Combining the search can help you to narrow the angle. Had she simply searched using the keyword 'boys' she would have found many thousands of articles, most unrelated to what she wished to look at.

Fundamental to a successful search is using the right key words so that enough of a clue is offered in the title to allow you to reject or pursue particular search results. If you don't get anything in your initial searches, try using synonyms to alter the keywords. It is not unusual for the initial enquiry to start quite wide, as Karen's did. Some articles might offer an excellent model that you want to measure your own teaching by, while others provide some quick insights into the area. Until you have conducted a search you will not to have a good enough grasp of how much research is out there. The quality of the research you cite is better than the quantity. So, it is legitimate to find an article describing a study in the area you are interested in and use that as the main piece of literature you measure your own findings by.

When Karen started to look for literature she found articles that provided a critical analysis of the English curriculum arguing it was very 'feminine' in book choices and approaches. She found articles based on studies of how teachers respond to boys in the classroom setting, and literature that described how boys excelled in certain areas of the curriculum which built on interactive learning approaches. From her reading she was able to get a sense of the ways in which boys' underachievement in writing had been debated.

Reading informs thinking

Karen's reading gave her some answers to some of her questions. The literature isn't enough of an answer, though; it would be easy to presume, based on reading alone, that if the problem wasn't unique to her but rather a large, wide-ranging one, then she need not worry about trying to do anything about it. It could simply lead her to a stalemate, legitimizing why the boys aren't working hard and rendering her powerless to do anything about it. Returning to Karen's original issue, however, should remind her that she wants to find ways of reducing the problem. Chapter 4 shows how to develop strategies for researching the classroom. In this chapter we now turn our attentions to what the Masters-level writing might look like.

Reflective Activity

Select three academic journal articles related to an area of teaching and learning which interests you. It may be something you are finding challenging or it may be something which is a strength you would like to develop.

Read through them each once to get a flavour of what they are about and then go back through them in more detail. Highlight areas which inform you about theory or research which underpins practice. Are there any contradictions between the papers in terms of the messages they are giving? What might be the reasons for these (e.g. sample size or type, school location, methods used, etc.)?

Now identify how the research in each of the papers may impact on your own practice. What could you change or develop and how will you monitor and evaluate the impact of these changes? Try them out and keep brief notes relating to what you changed and what effect it had.

Now consider how your reading and your evaluations have impacted on your practice. What more do you need to do to embed any changes? Is there further reading which would be helpful? Would it be useful to observe a more experienced colleague putting some of the approaches into practice?

Two case studies, starting with excellent!

Monique

Monique wanted to examine the theoretical and practical basis for supporting pupils who speak English as an additional language (EAL) in her classroom. Her study plan looked like this:

- Investigate the context of pupils speaking English as an additional language in the UK – what are the issues?

- Search for realistic models that can translate into classroom practice.

- Explore how these approaches can be integrated into a scheme of work.

- Evaluate the outcomes.

Monique had no prior experience of working with pupils who speak EAL but she did have experience in her degree study of how children acquire language and was broadly interested in the social issues attending to the area. She summarized that her main interests were: inclusion, and cultural diversity in teaching and learning and in how pupils can make progress. Monique made a decision at the beginning of her study not to view EAL speakers as a problem or 'deficit' category of students in her classroom but as potentially very capable language learners who frequently exceed the achievements of their monolingual peers. She had a hypothesis. Let's look at her opening paragraphs.

> Immigration to this country is nothing new, nor is the associated need to support children arriving in schools with little or no command of the English language as it is spoken in the classroom. As a nation we have received waves of immigration throughout our history. In the 1960s, for example, workers arrived from Commonwealth countries to set up new lives here, filling gaps in the labour market associated with Britain's prosperity at the time. Three generations later, these groups are British and many have never visited, nor intend visiting, the countries their grandparents left. The languages of their countries of origin have become termed 'community languages' and hybrid cultures and new dialects of English continue to emerge as ethnic groups intermingle in largely urban contexts.
>
> Today, with the enlargement of the EU, we see a new type of economic 'migrant' rather than 'immigrant', leaving home on a temporary basis to find work, sending money back and planning eventually to return. For this group, identity and focus remain firmly rooted in the country of origin, with technology and cheap air travel making it possible to maintain close links with family and friends left behind. As Harris et al. (2001) put it, 'social identity is increasingly "deterritorialized"'. In other words, national identity is a matter of choice and individual sensibility, rather than physical residency.

In these opening ideas Monique has set out a map of issues to be explored across the essay. She has connected with notions of history and context, different kinds of immigration and different language demands. Though she has only made use of one short quotation she has used it strategically to establish a clear thesis that the essay will explore issues of cultural and linguistic choice. Monique's essay continues to debate the different educational responses to supporting EAL pupils and to examine some models of support. By the end of the first review of the literature she has created a study design. It reads:

> Building on these theories and issues discussed above, in the next section I will look at how these might translate into strategies and tactics that can be adopted in the classroom to support the EAL pupil. In doing this I will follow the five principles suggested as guidelines by NALDIC.

Monique lists the guidelines and goes on to hypothesize:

> These principles both demystify much of the theory surrounding language learning and provide reassurance to most teachers that they are able to support the needs of those who speak English as an additional language. My contention is that a certain amount of explicit teaching will be required for *all* pupils to acquire appropriate language for the various curriculum subjects. I want to explore whether the teaching I do at an explicit level about language both supports the development of EAL users' confidence *and* improves the use of language by English speakers and users. Might all pupils benefit from greater focus on subject-specific, academic language and other strategies designed to support EAL pupils?

This paragraph completed the first half of a Masters-level assignment based on a review of theory and practice in EAL. Monique is able to shift her style now, from an objective third-person appraisal of theory to a first-person review of her own practice. This stylistic shift is an important one in Masters-level writing in education because it supports what this chapter and book have argued, that theoretical understanding will support practical outcomes. Monique has learned something about the field she has been studying through reading and analysis. Now, however, it is about her applying that to her own practice.

Here is the assignment feedback the tutor wrote for Monique:

> An *exceptionally good range* of literature was drawn upon to debate the area – focused on policy, practice and past and future issues. The studies drawn upon were *well explained and issues were debated fully. Your own search for the literature showed just how clear an idea you had of the complexity of the debate.* By Part 2 you had begun to critically apply the literature and showed a high level of understanding and appreciation.

> The sources have all been well explained, debated and critiqued. You set sources and viewpoints in context and systematically evaluated their worth. The time taken to contextualize the context of EAL pupils in UK built a good bridge between the theoretical and the practical.

A high level of understanding was evident throughout in terms of the principles of EAL support and the ways in which you made what often is expressed as an insurmountable problem of supporting EAL pupils, a manageable set of practical strategies that don't have to operate in a vacuum for lone pupils but are evidence of good language learning practice in general.

The assignment was exceptionally well written with a high standard of presentation and accurate referencing maintained throughout.

This is high-quality work that shows both a strong understanding of a complex issue and an informed approach to how to manage educational issues within the classroom environment. Excellent.

Overall the tutor was clearly pleased with Monique's assignment. What gets commended, though, shows how the relationship between theory and practice is always interwoven in terms of assessment. So, Monique's independence of thought, her systematic reviews of evidence and her application all receive positive comment. Monique has not developed her understanding of the theory as a separate entity to her practice but has drawn on the learning in the theory to inform her practice. It is important to note that Monique could write well and reference correctly and you should develop the style and approaches as part of your learning across the PGCE M-level year.

Chris (not everyone is as a good as Monique)

Chris did his whole-school study on behaviour management. He had decided to look at the reasons behind truancy rates. This in itself was not as well formed a scenario as the one Karen started out with. Chris did not have a plan, not even the basic plan that Monique worked from. His study touched upon an important local and national issue but he lacked a clear focus for what he wanted to explore. Truancy is, in fact, a wide-ranging problem and the reasons for pupils' truanting are varied – socio-economic disadvantage and difficulty at home, struggles with authority and behaviour and individual disenchantment. Chris hadn't broken down his first big term. When pressed for what he did want to concentrate on, Chris thought he would be able to base the whole study on conducting interviews with truants. He had not considered that there was an inherent flaw in such an approach: by the very nature of being truant, the children were not present to be interviewed! He had also not reflected sufficiently enough on the idea that, even when he did manage to interview pupils who truanted, he was not necessarily going to get a 'true' answer as to why they did skip school. Chris's study had problems.

- If he did not identify the background issues he could not research them very well.

- If he had not got a good enough sense of the theoretical field then he would struggle to devise good data-collecting strategies.

- The logistics of interviewing truants was vital.

- The ethical questions pertaining to this 'illicit' behaviour warranted a lot of thought in advance of the study.

Still he proceeded. Chris did have a hypothesis of sorts. He believed that there was nothing he could learn about truancy beyond what he asked people in his school and he could do that in an unsystematic way at any time he felt like it. The process of research requires some attention to rigour so that claims can be made for validity or reliability. That rigour can include much of what has been discussed in the previous case studies involving Karen and Monique. It requires a plan and a direction guided by questions. The answers to complex problems such as truancy won't appear as a 'vision' in front of you! You have to find them out. Chris presumed that asking questions in an ad hoc way in school would provide him with the answers he needed and little further work was necessary. Consequently, when he went to consult the 'literature', which, as in Karen's literature search, was a large body of work, he had no way of sorting through what was there. He opted to list some surface issues instead of researching in further detail. One of the difficulties with Chris's work was that he was unable to write in the critical, evaluative way expected for study at M-level.

 Activity

Try the self-assessment task in Table 5.2. Again, a few suggestions are given for targets to improve.

Table 5.2 Being a critical writer

Criteria The critical writer is able to:	Self-assessment rating: 1 = excellent 2 = good 3 = emerging skills 4 = skills yet to be acquired	Targets and date
Select evidence required for task		
Present subsidiary/associated information using correct grammatical structure		

Synthesize information from a variety of sources		For example: According to Author A (1995) pupils cannot sit still for a sustained period, whereas Author B (2006) refutes this claim as based on prejudice of teachers. There are a wide range of different theories.
Use subject-specific terminology		
Edit writing		Read – re-read.
Proof-read writing effectively		Use electronic support, but be careful with US software. Ask a friend to read for you.
Produce a coherent introduction which is not purely descriptive		
Interpret research data		Is the data significant – do you want to contest it? After all, asking six pupils doesn't prove much.
Synthesize the key points of the information, using your own language		Should come from your practice of the reading.
Evaluate the information		Should come from the reading.
Structure text using genre-specific rules		Use sub-headings to help you. Follow guidance given. Ask questions. Get feedback on drafts.
Cite references accurately		See guidance. Practise. Learn.
Produce a relevant and properly presented bibliography, using Harvard system		See guidance. Practise. Learn.

Chris's attempts to assemble his jumble of fact-finding into a coherent research report, following on from the issues raised in the planning stages, resulted in two sets of comments attached to his report. The comments referring to his resubmitted assignment are in italic.

Assignment feedback

Analysis of literature and research:

There are a number of references to relevant resources but the treatment of literature is often very superficial, e.g. simply quoting material as a way of saying things, or even just inserting material without analysis or other comment. Headings are offered, without examination, as classifications, causes and cures for truancy, so that critical consideration of issues in any depth is lacking. No argument or hypothesis has been developed from the reading.

Synthesis and utilization of evidence:

Describes the school's anti-truanting policy and system (sources not indicated and no linkage with literature) and gathers evidence by interviewing purposefully the behavioural coordinator and, less purposefully, three pupils. The data coming from these sources is reported, but the analysis is very limited and there is no linkage of the evidence with ideas in the literature.

The interviews conducted with the pupils remain under-exploited. The interviews only have value as a methodology if the candidate uses them to illustrate significant ideas already raised in the literature. The pupils' words are summarized, rather than used as a way of exemplifying ideas raised in the literature.

Structure:

Meanings sometimes unclear through uncompleted sentences.

This was much better written – clearer in expression and had been proof-read. However, there are still errors in the work. Notably the text remains written in the future tense rather than the past tense: 'I will conduct interviews' rather than showing that the work has taken place.

Presentation:

Very frequent errors of expression in the text. Much more thorough proof-reading needed.

In summary, the resubmission did show improvement but not sufficient to attain the minimum grade for a Masters-level pass.

Chris's tutor identified a number of problems. Chris had done some reading but had separated what he had learned in the reading from what relevance it had to the rest of the study. He had inadvertently rendered the reading useless. By treating the academic study as an additional pressure he has not made the connection intellectually that the purpose of the study is for him to strengthen his understanding of truancy and, crucially, how to find strategies to respond to truancy. Because he hadn't thought the knowledge could be valuable to him, he had struggled to find it.

The fundamental problems with planning in the early stages exist throughout the work. Chris hadn't sufficiently researched the reasons why children truant. He had gained some knowledge, because, as the tutor comments, he had listed some reasons why pupils might truant. However, those reasons lacked qualification from the theoretical base. What will be important for Chris to know – especially as he has tried to find out directly from pupils – is why this particular school had an issue with truancy and what they might have done about it. Though he had sought some direct answers from some truants he had identified, he hadn't really shown what he had found out through those interviews nor what wider issues were revealed by those interviews. Chris had separated out each of the categories of assessment into individual responses and his overall report lacked cohesion. Where Karen had learned something new she could put into place and Monique had trialled a specific approach to evaluate its worth, Chris hadn't done anything that was very useful to his wider knowledge. For it to be valuable – to join up theory and practice – you need to think in terms of exploring questions that you think will be of use to you! The idea of worthiness and value is explored further in Chapter 4.

Writing well

Monique was a mature student with prior industry experience in publishing and she was able to adapt those skills easily to the academic frame. All kinds of different students appear on PGCE M-level courses: mature candidates who haven't written formally for many years, some undergraduates with varying degrees of confidence, and some who have specific problems with writing. Tutors don't expect that the style will always be consistent but there are some conventions of writing that need to be learned. It is not easy for all candidates to adopt the academic model right away.

One academic outcome of studying at Masters level is that, for some candidates, it can be the beginning of a much larger journey into academic learning. For many on PGCE M-level courses, at least initially, it is an outcome and a demand on top of everything else. The conventions for writing at Masters usually follow a predominantly academic model, founded on the notion that research has the potential to inform further thinking and debate more widely. In short, the work should be presented in a publishable form, with due attention paid to the works cited following a common structure of academic referencing.

In an extended piece of research, like an MPhil or PhD, or as commonly seen in an academic book, authors will provide a full bibliography, that is a list of all books and articles consulted in order to write the book. A Masters piece of research is better served by a reference list where you would use the Harvard referencing system to provide an alphabetically ordered list of all the texts that were explicitly cited or quoted in the report. A reference list entry might look like this:

Author Surname, Author Initial (Year of Publication) *Title of Book* or 'Title of article'. Place of publication: Publisher.

Generally the author's name appears first, surname before initial, followed by the year the book/article was published. You need to make some distinction in the punctuation between a book (it might be underlined or in italic) and an article ('in inverted commas'). The place of publication and the publisher complete the reference. There are variations and differences with citing books (whether single-authored, co-authored or edited) and articles and some inconsistencies in citing web-sites and some professional literature. If you are in any doubt, ask you college or university for further guidance or use a reference list from a reputable published book as a model. Often what is most important is that you use a system consistently.

How does academic writing at M-level make me a better teacher?

Karen's problems earlier in this chapter represent a familiar set of concerns felt by both beginner and more experienced teachers in classrooms. That Karen followed through her problems and sought answers beyond the school – through reviews of literature, analyses of perspectives and close examination of her own approaches – gave her power to resolve her own issues. Equally, Monique developed a closely designed classroom study from an extensive critical review of support for EAL pupils. So what?

The purpose of academic learning is not to separate those that know from those that have yet to find out. Teachers becoming part of an academic community through Masters level work enter into a world where sharing knowledge is valued. Through the processes of writing and, in time, through publishing, new knowledge about teaching and learning is spread. Through this kind of dissemination we all learn to become much better teachers and active players in solving the day-to-day problems of classrooms.

Summary

This chapter explored the ways in which you can develop your academic writing style. The most daunting aspect of this area of the course is the production of an extended essay yet the actual writing of the essay is a much smaller element than creating that essay. Writing at M-level is a cyclical process that begins with some reflections on problems, hypothesizing and organizing questions, reading, thinking, writing, redrafting. Each of these stages of the writing process is continuously informed by being open to new insights through reading, reflecting and thinking. Learning to read critically will help you to write critically, and this will only come through accessing a range of reading. Using the literature sources available to you is a good start and access to electronic resources has certainly helped students to organize their time more effectively and efficiently and to read widely. You already have a good starting point in that you have proved your ability to write at a higher academic level in your first degree even if for some of you that was some time ago. As an enthusiastic new teacher hypothesizing should come easy with careful reflections, each day as a teacher you will face new problems and challenges. Combining your curiosity to improve with a systematic approach to problem-solving should set you in very good stead to achieve your PGCE at M-level. Good luck!

Further reading

Department of Education at: http://www.education.gov.uk. The key portal to all central government education and children services developments.

National Association for Language Development in the Curriculum (NALDIC) at: http://www.naldic.org.uk/. A valuable resource for those supporting children with English as an additional language.

Ofsted at: http:// www.ofsted.gov.uk. The central site for the inspecting body of education and children's services. Provides access to all current school and teacher training institution Ofsted reports.

Subject association websites, e.g. the Association for Science Education at: http:// www.ase. org.uk. Subject websites provide a breadth of support for trainee and experienced teachers. They often require membership but this will give access to resources, conferences, fora, etc.

Wyse, D. (2012) *The Good Writing Guide for Education Students*, 3rd edn. London: Sage. A useful guide to help you structure and develop your writing to meet the demands of writing at Masters level.

6 Getting a job with a PGCE at M-level

Keira Sewell

Historically the PGCE has always been a professional award and anecdotal evidence shows that many employers have yet to recognize the difference between the PGCE H-level and the PGCE M-level. Therefore it is up to you to ensure that potential employers understand what additional qualities you have to offer as an applicant. This chapter aims to help you to do this by:

- helping you make decisions about the kind of job you should apply for in your first teaching post;

- supporting you in filling in the application form and structuring a letter of application in a way which will make you stand out from other applicants for the post and enable you to make the best of the M-level element of your programme of study;

- exploring the factors you need to consider when planning a sample lesson for use in the interview process;

- helping you prepare for the interview.

So how do I sell myself to potential employers?

The first thing you need to think about is how to choose which jobs to apply for. Remember that wherever you apply, the school will already have in mind the sort of person they feel will complement their existing staff team. They may be looking specifically for a younger member of staff if a number of the existing teachers are approaching retirement age; they may be in need of a specific subject specialism or skill such as playing the piano or coaching the football team, or they may be looking for a certain personality. While some of these things are obvious from the job specification, others are much harder to determine.

Probably the best strategy is to apply only for those jobs you really want. This can seem really difficult if you are beginning to feel that 'your' job will never come along but enthusiasm for a job is palpable and definitely comes across (or not) through application forms and interviews. If you go into an interview feeling half-hearted, it will show. Reflect for a while on what kind of job you are really looking for. It is likely that you will stay in your first teaching post for at least two years; you want to do this in a place which meets your personal and professional needs. Think about the following:

- Where do you want/need to work for personal reasons? Do you need to look in a certain area, near where you live, or do you mind commuting long distances? Personally I would not want to teach in the area in which I live; you do feel you are on show to both pupils and parents even during time out from school. It always amuses me how pupils and parents seem shocked at the fact that teachers do not live in their store cupboards, but have to shop, eat, socialize and have leisure time along with 'normal' people!

- What kind of a school do you want to work in? Would you prefer a large urban/suburban school or a smaller rural school? Are you looking for a primary/infant/junior school or an 11–16/11–18 comprehensive?

- What interests do you have in terms of education and to what extent do you want to be able to pursue these through the post? This should include reflection on your aspirations for further study and the opportunities for this offered in the school context. For example, if you are particularly interested in pupils for whom English is an additional language then try to target your search for a teaching post which provides opportunities to engage in study in this area.

- What kind of challenges do you want in your first teaching post? At some schools managing pupil behaviour is a major challenge; some schools have higher academic expectations than others, while certain schools see themselves at the cutting edge of education and are regular instigators of new practice.

Having spotted your perfect job, read through the advertisement carefully. If it states 'Experienced teacher required' then it is unlikely they are intending to employ a newly qualified teacher. This should not necessarily put you off but you should be aware that you would be at a disadvantage. Similarly, if the advert says 'teaching to A level' and you have no experience of this, you will need to make a good case to be considered. Age phase is often not quite so important in primary teaching. Although an advert may say 'Key Stage 1 teacher required', there is some scope for moving teachers around year groups if you can bring a real strength to the teaching team.

When you have sent for details, study the job specification closely. What essential and/or desirable characteristics are they looking for and how will they determine whether you have them? For example, if they are looking for a French specialist and they will determine this from the application form, ensure that you make this clear either on the form itself and/or in your letter of application. If it is essential to have experience of teaching A-level science and you have taught only to GCSE level it is unlikely that you will be shortlisted if other candidates have this experience. (I know from my own experience, however, that if the job is really the one you want, sometimes you may be able to convince an employer that you are the right person for them.)

Read through the information sent to you about the school and visit their website for more details to see if you can find out about the school's philosophy. Look at the academic qualifications of the head teacher, which are often on the letterhead or on the website. If they have a Masters award, for instance, they may value the academic element you can bring with you (although you should not rely on this as the sole indication!) Read the most recent Ofsted report and find out if the school promotes professional development of its staff, particularly if you would like to continue your studies in the future. Do an Internet search on the name of the school – this may reveal further information. A friend of mine once did this, only to find that the school she was applying to was due to close in two years' time! If you can, visit the school and have a look round. I find that you can tell a lot about a school simply by walking into the reception area. Ask any questions you may have, but the fact that you are looking round the school will contribute to the selection and recruitment process so think carefully about how you phrase these to ensure you do not prejudice your chances. One head teacher told me about an applicant who they felt demonstrated a lack of commitment to the school during an initial visit by asking what time teachers left at the end of the school day. Although it may seem legitimate to discover what expectations the school would have of your time, it is probably better to drive past the school in an evening and see how many cars are still in the car park.

Filling out the application form

Having found the right job and checked that you can fulfil all of the essential criteria, or as many of the desirable criteria as possible, you need to complete the application form. Look carefully at the instructions. If it does not ask you to include a curriculum vitae then you are best not doing so. Although most application forms can now be submitted online, some still require you to write them by hand. Some applications also ask you not to submit a letter in addition to the application form but rather to write/type any additional information in the space provided. There are different views on this: I always submit an additional letter; however, some head teachers will automatically ignore anything over and above the application form. Unfortunately there is no way of telling what will get you noticed, but it is important that any potential employer has the opportunity to see what you consider to be the best of you. If you feel a letter of application does this most effectively then include one: there is little you can do if they choose to ignore it, but do you want to work for them anyway?

Proof-read your application very carefully: spelling mistakes or typographical errors suggest to an employer that you are not fully committed to the post. I often find it useful to complete a 'practice' form first. Ensure that all sections are complete and that you have used as few acronyms as possible. When completing the qualifications section, write out your award title in full, for example Postgraduate Certificate in Education. You can put further information in brackets – (60 credit points at Masters level) – and don't forget to indicate somewhere that you have Qualified Teacher Status.

When it comes to the personal statement or letter of application, this is where you can really sell your M-level work. Here are two examples of opening paragraphs:

 Sarah

I am currently completing the secondary PGCE at the University at the End of the World, specializing in English, and I would like to apply for the English position at your school. During my training I have had experience in three different schools and have successfully completed all my placements. I am strongly committed to the teaching profession and feel my experiences have enabled me to develop a number of strengths which I can bring with me to the post.

 Liam

I am currently completing the secondary Postgraduate Certificate in Education, specializing in English, at the University at the End of the World, a programme of study which has enabled me to reflect on the integration of theory, practice and research and to engage critically with current thinking in education. As part of this programme I completed two modules at Masters level. The first enabled me to analyse research and theory around a pedagogical issue and the second enabled me to engage in a piece of small-scale research to consider how practitioner research can contribute to the development of best practice in the secondary classroom. As I have a keen interest in the use of drama in developing skills in speaking and listening, I chose to reflect critically on the ways in which this approach can support pupils' development. A review of the literature suggested that drama has a key role in this aspect of pupil understanding, specifically in encouraging a range of perspectives and enabling pupils to debate at a high level, and I chose to develop this idea through a small-scale research project of my own. The findings from my research indicated that the key strengths of role play are the ways in which it develops independent thought, encourages critical evaluation and promotes research and critical reflection. However, my research also demonstrated that the management of this approach is complex and that careful planning and sensitive delivery and organization are required in order to maximize effectiveness. I found this research invaluable in informing my practice in the classroom and look forward to utilizing it further with my own class. On a broader level, I have found developing my own critical thinking and levels of analysis, through reflection on theory, research and practice, to be an invaluable part of my development as a beginning teacher and I know that my desire for knowledge and understanding of both the subject level and the pedagogy which underpins good practice will enable me to continue to develop as a teacher throughout my career.

Now consider the following:

- What do you now know about each of these candidates?

- Who would you choose to interview and why?

- What will each of them bring to your school?

- Who may have greater impact on pupil learning?

- Which letter do you want to read more of?

Hopefully you would be more inclined to interview Liam than Sarah. Liam tells us much more about what his course entailed, and he writes well, not merely describing but explaining the ways in which his course has contributed to his professional development. Most of all, you want to know more about what this person has been doing and how it has evolved. This is important if you are to present yourself as the critical, evaluative, analytical and original thinking professional who would be an asset to any school. Remember that everyone leaving initial teacher education will have the professional knowledge and understanding, attributes and skills appropriate to a beginning teacher, otherwise they would not have achieved the Professional Standards and gained Qualified Teacher Status. It is *your* job to tell potential employers about *your* strengths, and one of these must be the level of thinking required to study successfully at Masters level.

How do you then continue in this frame? Let us look at the next paragraph.

 Liam

As part of my training I have had experience in three schools, all of which were different in terms of intake, size and philosophy. This experience has enabled me to identify those things which I would wish to take forward in my own teaching. First, I have a strong commitment to enabling all pupils to reach their full potential as learners. This requires careful planning which allows for personalization of learning within a framework which is manageable for the teacher. Allowing some autonomy can often be an effective way of implementing this, perhaps providing the opportunity for pupils to choose an area of interest as the focus for their studies through a common framework which enables assessment criteria to be met. For example, one boy in my class found report-writing extremely difficult until I changed the context to writing the weekly match report of his own football team. His interest was evident through the improvements in motivation, behaviour and achievement. While this adaptation to the lesson focus is relatively minor, the PGCE M-level has enabled me to synthesize my understanding of theory and research and my knowledge of the statutory requirements of the curriculum in order to solve problems creatively. As a beginning teacher, I am sure that I will be required to adapt my teaching throughout my career to meet the challenges brought both by the changing needs of pupils and by the changing curricula requirements and initiatives. I feel that the PGCE programme has prepared me effectively for my future career.

What Liam does well is tell us something about what he believes to be important and he provides an example through which he can express his understanding of the theories and research which have helped frame his thinking. He indicates his flexibility within the classroom and his willingness to get to know the pupils and to incorporate their interests, ideas or expertise. He shows us that he is aware of his responsibilities to the curriculum and the strategies and agendas which underpin this, so we do not get the impression that he is a complete maverick, willing to throw the National Curriculum in the bin for 'the good of all pupils'; rather, we understand that he has learned how to interpret the curriculum in a way which promotes learning. He also demonstrates that he understands that he will continue to face challenges throughout his career and that he is prepared for the changes which will inevitably face him. There is also a sense that he is in teaching long term as he is already thinking beyond the first year.

It would not be appropriate for all of us to write letters like Liam. Essentially, the key lies in identifying what you feel is most important to you and then setting about conveying this in a way which tells us *why* you think it is important, *what* has informed your thinking and *how* it has influenced your practice. Obviously you will have thoughts about a number of areas so try to incorporate two or three examples which exemplify your key ideas. When you have chosen these, consider the following:

- What pedagogy underpins my thinking? What is my philosophy?

- Why do I think this is important? Is it because of something that happened to me or an experience I have had in school?

- What reading, research, experiences, policies, strategies have helped to frame this?

- What have I done in school which exemplifies my thinking?

- What evidence do I have of the impact my teaching has had on children's learning?

Always ensure that your letter is specific to the school. It is time-consuming to write individual letters of application, but a churned out standard letter is very obvious to potential employers. Hopefully, if you get it right you will not need to write too many anyway. On a practical level, letters of application should usually be no longer than two sides. However interesting your letter is, some unfortunate head teacher on the other end will be wading their way through piles of applications and trying to choose those they will put on the shortlist. One school I know had 120 applications for one post and the head teacher had to use every strategy to reduce this to a shortlist of ten – not an easy task!

 Activity

Look at the job specification in Table 6.1 and complete the second column to show what experiences/qualifications/interests you could include to demonstrate that you meet the criteria required.

Table 6.1 Exemplar person specification

Essential characteristics	Ways in which I could demonstrate this
Education and training	
Degree level or equivalent	
Qualified teacher status	
Relevant experience	
A current and broad knowledge and understanding of the primary curriculum	
Experience in specific key stage or year group	
Professional knowledge and skills	
A good understanding of positive behaviour management systems	

The ability to plan, prepare, provide and evaluate activities that promote learning	
The ability to monitor and record whole-class and individual progress effectively and to use this information to support continued progress	
Commitment to taking an active role within the school, including assemblies, staff and INSET meetings and in-school policy-making	
Commitment to personal responsibility for keeping up to date with developments in education and the curriculum	
Additional factors	
A good sense of humour	
A flexible approach to all aspects of school life	
The ability to work both independently and as a member of a team	
The ability to manage and work alongside other adults in the same classroom	

Planning a sample lesson

In recent years, requiring applicants to teach a short lesson has become accepted practice. It is a useful part of the recruitment process and allows schools at least a snapshot into whether someone can 'walk the walk' as well as 'talk the talk'.

Sometimes you will be told what area they wish you to teach, at others you will be free to choose. If you are applying for a secondary post then you will usually be asked to teach your specialist subject and given a particular focus for the lesson, but in primary schools it may be completely up to you. Both these approaches have their advantages and disadvantages and personal preference varies. Whichever is the case, you need to think first about why sample lessons have become such a popular component of the recruitment process. Before you plan your lesson, consider what the school wants to achieve in providing you with an opportunity to demonstrate your teaching. The following questions may be useful in framing your thinking.

- What do you think are your strengths and how could you incorporate these into your lesson?

- What areas do you know present challenges and how could you avoid these?

- What aspects does the job description say will be identified through the interview process and how could you incorporate these into your lesson?

- How nervous do you think you might be and how could you structure your lesson to ease this?

- What resources are available in the classroom (e.g. ICT, access to an outdoor area) and what resources would you need to take with you?

- What age group are you expected to teach and how can you demonstrate understanding of this in your plan?

- How long will the lesson last and realistically what can you achieve in this time?

- How does your lesson promote learning and how would you know if this has been achieved?

- What did you say about your own philosophy of teaching and learning in your application and how can you demonstrate this in practice?

- What is the school most proud of in terms of teaching and learning and how can you demonstrate that you would be able to 'carry the torch'?

Consider the case of Halima. She is delighted to be invited for interview to teach in Key Stage 2 at the local primary school. She has not been given a focus for the lesson which will last 30 minutes, but she knows she will teach a Year 5 class.

Although nervous about the teaching element of the interview, she would like to use the opportunity to demonstrate some of her strengths which she feels include using the interactive whiteboard (IWB), positive behaviour management, creativity and integrated curriculum planning. Therefore she wants to choose an area which will enable her to demonstrate these elements and decides on an activity which involves space travel.

Halima plans a lesson which begins with a look at an interactive website where the requirements for healthy plant growth are explored. She gets four different pupils up to use the website and through this ensures that the pupils are clear about the requirements. She then gives each group a selection of 'leaves' from the planet Xag and tells them she has recently been on holiday there. The pupils are asked to discuss what they know about the planet, based on the leaves in front of them. Each group then feeds back to the whole class and Halima records their ideas on the whiteboard.

She has planned this activity for a number of reasons. First it enables her to demonstrate confidence in using the IWB in two different ways. Getting the pupils up to use the interactive website means she shows her willingness to involve the pupils; it also gives her time to refer to her plan to ensure she is eliciting the areas of learning outlined on it. She knows she writes well on the IWB and uses this method to record the pupils' ideas, as she is aware there will be little time for individual writing. Secondly, it demonstrates her creativity in integrating science, ICT and English. This activity could be the starting point for a number of activities covering a range of subjects. Thirdly, the context of the planet Xag is a useful approach for Halima as she likes using humour as a way of establishing relationships with her pupils. She is able to tell them stories about her visit there as a means of engaging their interest and reducing poor behaviour resulting from a lack of motivation. She is hoping that they will laugh at some of her stories and that this response will help to calm her nerves. Fourthly, the activity can be extended to suit the time available, an important factor when working with an unknown group. Finally, the mix of whole-class and small-group activities allows her to demonstrate a range of behaviour management strategies and her skills in interacting with both groups.

It is critical that Halima thinks about both *what* she will teach and *why*, as this will enable her to demonstrate her developing professional knowledge and understanding, her skills and attributes and her understanding of current thinking in education. It is likely that she will be asked about her choice of lesson during the interview and with careful thought she can prepare well for this question.

Being interviewed

'What will they ask me?' trainees often want to know. The answer is usually: 'It depends what they want from the person seeking the post.' There are good clues in the job description. If the criteria indicate that evidence will be gained from the interview it is likely you will get questions in these areas.

For example, if one of the job description requirements is 'the ability to work both independently and as part of a team' it is likely you will be asked how you have done this in previous jobs or during your training. This could be a direct question, requiring you to give an example, or you could be offered a scenario question such as: 'You are working alongside a colleague in the same year group to plan the activities for your pupils. How would you ensure that this is a joint partnership?'

There are several key areas which are often included in the questions asked by the panel, for example inclusion, behaviour management, Every Child Matters, planning and assessment, and the inevitable 'Why do you want to work at this school?' Again, you should read the school details sent to you carefully and demonstrate in your answers that you have at least accessed their website.

Activity

It is impossible to predict the specific questions you will be asked, as all panels phrase these differently. However, it may help you to develop responses to the following:

- Why are you applying for this particular post?

- If you were a pupil in your class, what would you say about your teacher's strengths and weaknesses?

- How would you integrate a child with English as an additional language who has moved into your class?

- How do you promote excellence and enjoyment in your work as a teacher?

- What would Assessment for Learning look like in your classroom? What would you do to address the needs of a child you identified as not meeting their potential?

- Give the panel an example of one behaviour management strategy you have used successfully.

- Pupil voice is extremely important to us as a school. How would you listen to pupils' views and implement their ideas into your practice.

- What do you think will be the key changes in education over the next five years?

- Where would you like to be in your career in ten years' time?

- What subject area would you be interested in leading and why?

- You are walking along the corridor at change of lessons and you see a fight happening. One of the pupils says he is being bullied by the other, something which is vigorously denied by the other child. You are due to teach in five minutes. What would you do?

Remember that the questions are designed to elicit information from you, to tell the interviewers something about who you are and what you believe in. The second question is specifically designed to find out something about you. Initially it appears to want to know what your strengths and areas for development are, but it is also designed to explore your self-perceptions. There is a fine balance in developing a good answer to this question. If you spend five minutes telling the panel what you do badly and one minute telling them what you do well they are likely to believe that you are indicating that you have lots of weaknesses. If, however, you spend some time explaining what you do well and then say that you cannot really think of something you do badly they may think you are overconfident and unwilling to learn from others. Remember that you have already identified your strengths and the areas you need to develop in your Career Entry Development Profile (CEDP); use this as the basis of your response. But also remember that you do have to blow your own trumpet a little as no one else is going to do it for you.

The last question is slightly different as it is phrased as a scenario. Although at first sight the question may seem to focus on a very practical response, this is the moment to demonstrate your knowledge of the theories and research which underpin practice, and you should use the opportunity to the full. First, they are trying to find out if you understand teachers' roles and responsibilities. You have a responsibility to support the welfare of all pupils in the school so your answer should reflect this by showing that you are clear that some action should be taken and that it is not an option to simply ignore the incident because the pupils are not in any of your classes. Secondly, they want to know if you understand the role of the pastoral welfare system and the ways in which this underpins both pupil welfare and pupil discipline. Therefore they are looking for an answer which includes both your initial response and referral to the pastoral system of the school. Thirdly, they are checking that you have an understanding of the management of bully/victim problems. You may wish, therefore, to refer to theory and research in this area by talking about the complexities of bullying, the fact that it cannot be resolved in the five minutes that you have before going to teach and the strategies available to support you. In being aware of the purpose of questions during an interview, you can show that you are capable of critical evaluation and the ability to apply your developing knowledge and understanding in situations which are both complex and sensitive.

It is important to remember that there is often no right or wrong way to answer interview questions, and the questions will have been designed to discover whether you will fit in with the philosophy of the school and the staff already there. Bearing this in mind it is important that you answer honestly. After all, you can only be yourself in your job and if your philosophies, beliefs, values and attitude do not fit with the school's interpretation of what they want/need then this is not the right place for you. It may be useful to bring examples of your work to the interview, perhaps extracted from the portfolio you have used to evidence the Professional Standards during your training, to illustrate your responses, but remember that the panel will not have time to look at everything you have brought. It is not a good idea to ask them to go through everything.

If you have taught a lesson as part of the process then it is likely you will be asked something about this, for example 'Why did you choose the area or the approach?' This is where you can really demonstrate your M-levelness. Halima would be able to draw on research about effective use of the IWB, the theories which underpin effective behaviour management or the role of creativity and current initiatives in this area.

At the end of the interview you will have the opportunity to ask the panel questions. This is not the time to ask about holidays or how much they are going to pay you. Good questions can focus on the support they offer you during the induction year, the extent of the responsibilities attached to the post, opportunities for career development or clarification of anything which remains unclear following the visit. This is also an appropriate time to explore potential for pursuing further study if this is your aim.

You will usually be asked whether you would take up the position should you be offered it. I always find this a difficult question; it takes real nerve to say no to a panel at this point. However, if you really feel the post is not for you then you should say so as this frees them to consider the other candidates.

Some schools include an interview by the pupils themselves. This can be a formal session, perhaps conducted by members of the school council, or it can be quite informal, perhaps by pupils showing you round the school. This is a good opportunity for you to put into practice your understanding of theory and research around pupil perception and voice. For example, research tells us that pupils much prefer a teacher who is 'firm but fair' to one who is either very relaxed, almost buddy-like, or very strict. Pupils pick up signals about what kind of a teacher you would be very quickly and this will inform their judgement of you. Therefore telling them you just want to be their 'mate' may not be the best approach; however, giving them examples of how you have involved pupils in your teaching may be a good way of conveying to them what you feel is important.

After the interview

Schools vary considerably in the methods used to inform candidates and the length of time it takes. Some will telephone everyone, whether you are successful or not, others will write to you with the outcome. However they choose to do this, try and seek feedback. It is unlikely that you will be in the right state of mind to do so if you get the news over the phone, particularly if this is on the day of interview; ask if you can telephone back in a few days' time for information on why you were not successful. Feedback will enable you to identify any areas you can improve for your next interview. Remember, if you do not get the job try not to get disheartened, it is more than likely that the post was not right for you and that you will be better off elsewhere.

Reflective Activity

Often you will hear people say they like (or don't like) the feel of a school even when all they have done is to walk into the reception area. For this activity, try to visit a school, or use your current placement school if this is not possible. You are going to walk into it as someone who wants to understand its ethos and philosophy rather than as a trainee teacher or prospective employee.

What do your first impressions of the school tell you about it? Are there clues in the spaces around the school, in the work displayed on walls, in awards and achievements in the reception area, in photographs? What do you feel these clues tell you about the school's approach to learning? Go into some of the classrooms. What do you like/dislike about them? Are there things which you would like to emulate in your own classroom?

Reflective Activity

We often talk about creating a safe and secure learning environment in which achievement is supported and successes celebrated but, in reality, how we do this is often difficult to identify. Read the overview of one project's outcomes in identifying the elements of an 'ethos of achievement' reported at http://www.hmie.gov.uk/documents/publication/eoa-01.htm. Now try to identify what elements you have seen in the clues in your wander around the school.

Identify four things that you will do in your classroom to promote an ethos of achievement. Use these when you write your personal statement and when you go for interview. It will demonstrate that you are thinking not only about what you want to achieve but also how you will achieve it.

Summary

If reading this chapter has not put you off applying for jobs completely, then the following may help you prepare.

- Which area do you want to teach in and what factors have influenced your choice? Are there some factors on which you would be prepared to compromise?

- What kind of school do you want to teach in and why?

- What age phase is your preferred choice and why?

- To what extent can you fulfil the essential and desirable criteria set out in the job description?

- What do you already know about the school and where can you find out more?

- What do you feel are your particular strengths and how can you best communicate these at both selection and interview to a potential employer?

- How can you ensure that you make best use of the knowledge, understanding and transferable skills developed through the M-levelness of the PGCE?

- Do you have other skills, expertise or experience beyond the PGCE which may support your application?

- What hints or pointers are there in the interview details or the school information about the sorts of questions the school may ask you at interview?

- What else do you need to know in order to make an informed decision about whether to take up the post should you be offered it?

Finally, happy job hunting and good luck!

Further reading

Griff, T. (2010) 'How to get shortlisted for a teaching job', *Times Educational Supplement*, 1 September. Online at: http://www.tes.co.uk/article.aspx?storycode=6008055. Provides a very useful insight into what schools want, with examples, for those applying for their first teaching post.

Probationer Teacher Scotland, applying for jobs in Scotland. Online at: http://www.probationerteacherscotland.org.uk/hints-and-tips/job-hunting/applying-for-jobs.aspx. Provides some very helpful hints and tips for those seeking their first post in Scotland.

Ward, H. (2010) 'Getting a job', in G. Birrell, H. Taylor and H. Ward, *Succeeding on Your Primary PGCE*. London: Sage.

The *Times Educational Supplement* is a useful reference point for current issues in education and in reviewing some of the teaching posts being offered around the country. TES Connect (http://www.tes.co.uk) also provides access to a range of downloadable resources and a job search facility.

Local authority websites will also give details of current vacancies.

7 Continuing your studies

Keira Sewell

Completing the PGCE M-level is not the end of the journey in becoming a teacher but rather just another section of the journey completed. Hopefully you will continue to learn and develop as a teacher throughout your career, and you need to consider how best to do this. This chapter aims to:

- explore why continuing your studies will support your developing professionalism;

- explain the options available to you;

- explain how you can transfer your Masters-level credits into further study;

- help you decide on which course you should choose;

- help you decide when you should continue your studies;

- explore solutions to potential barriers to further study.

Why should I continue my studies?

In a recent survey I conducted with my PGCE students I asked whether they would choose to continue their M-level study into a Masters award-bearing course and to state the reasons for their choice. Eighty-two per cent of the students indicated that they would choose to continue their studies, many stating that they would consider it 'a waste not to'. One reply, however, took me a little by surprise. This student said they would not consider doing a Masters award as they 'never wanted to study education again'. Although I can understand the sentiments of a student who had just completed a very intensive and demanding programme, I was concerned to think that someone going into the teaching profession would not consider themselves as continually engaged in 'studying education'. Perhaps therefore, it is the notion of *studying* which needs exploring a little further.

There is no doubt that if you are to keep up with the pace of educational change you will need to reflect on your own practice and the way in which you are supporting the educational development of the pupils in your care. At its most basic, this is a requirement of being an effective teacher. The danger in this, however, is that we resort to 'navel-gazing', continually looking inwards to ourselves and our own classrooms and never once raising our heads to see the broader landscape. If we did this, education would never move forward, but would always be based in the descriptive, anecdotal references of 'I've always done it like this and it seems to work' rather than critical, analytical references: 'Why do I do it like this?' 'Why does it work?' 'Would it work better if I did it differently?' Think about the use of the interactive whiteboard (IWB) as an example.

The IWB has been a fantastic addition to the strategies we can employ to support teaching and learning, however, there are already indications that pupils are becoming bored with its use and that it is failing to continue to promote the 'Wow' factor from its introduction. We need to face the fact head on that our pupils are much more technologically advanced than we are. They are growing up in a world in which technology is fast-moving and highly challenging. How many of you get your own children to sort out your DVD recorder or your mobile phone, and how many know of children who, when using a new computer program, never refer to the manual but simply press buttons to find out what happens? To someone who remembers (and was fascinated by) the first computer game to be played through the television, the world of computer graphics now available seems a long way off from the days I was transfixed by playing computer tennis in my friend's living room!

As a medium for teaching, the IWB introduced a high-tech, highly visual resource into the classroom. It can be used to captivate and motivate pupils, but does it promote learning? The answer to this is complex but relies on the same questions as could be asked about any other type of teaching resource or strategy. It is only unique in that it presents a different type of medium, not that learning or teaching is necessarily radically changed by its use. In order for it to promote learning effectively we need to explore how and why it could potentially be used and emerging research in this area is beginning to identify how this can be achieved. This research is also identifying ways in which the IWB can be further developed to continue to be an effective resource: in other words it is informing our future direction as well as leading current developments. Without reference to this research, IWBs will become dinosaurs within the classroom, with pupils moving way beyond the technology offered by its usage. For this reason alone, further study is a necessity rather than an option for *all* teachers.

Study does not necessarily lead to academic qualifications. It is a requirement that all trainees completing their initial teacher education should prepare a Career Entry Development Profile (CEDP). This provides the basis for the areas you need to develop during your induction period, with the support of your school mentor, and meeting these targets will require you to engage with theory, research and practice in these areas. However, development does not end once you have met your induction targets; all teachers should engage with professional development throughout their career, whether this means attending a staff meeting which explores the effectiveness of behaviour management strategies within the school, applying for a local authority delivered course on assessment, training which supports their subject knowledge and understanding, or simply reading education-related literature. Training can lead to professional qualifications, such as the National Professional Qualification for Headship (NPQH), first-aid training, counselling or coaching certificates. The nature of teaching is such that you will never know everything about teaching and learning (and sometimes you will feel you know nothing at all!). Indeed the time to leave the profession is when you feel you have nothing left to learn. It is, therefore, a prerequisite for entering teaching that you will be engaged in some kind of further study.

Whether you decide to continue academic study or not is largely a matter of personal choice. Hopefully, however, you will have enjoyed the challenge offered by thinking at this level and have seen the benefits of a deepening understanding of the relationship between theory, research and practice and will choose to continue at some point in the future.

Reflective Activity

We often focus on the things we feel are our weaknesses. This can lead to a plateau in the areas where we are stronger. For this activity you will need to identify one area in which you feel you have made significant improvements and developed real strengths during your time on the PGCE. This could be behaviour management, planning, assessment, meeting the needs of individual learners, etc.

Now reflect on the elements which have enabled you to make these changes. It is likely to have been a combination of factors such as watching more experienced teachers, reading about how children learn, reading research articles which focus on this aspect, reading professional papers or articles.

Consider now how you could continue to develop your practice in this area. What do you need to do next and how will you ensure your continued professional development? Identify up to five things you will do in the coming year to develop your thinking in this field. These should include at least one reference each to research, theory and practice.

What further study options are available?

As part of your induction period you should have access to a range of training opportunities. These will include a half day provided for NQT training which will sometimes be in-school and sometimes external or local authority-led. This time is highly beneficial in enabling you to address the targets identified in your CEDP and developed further with your mentor during induction. Watching other teachers teach, working with subject leaders in your school, visiting other schools and talking with NQTs in your region are all important aspects of your continuing professional development. Staff meetings in school and in-service training days will also help you embed some of the theories, policies and strategies in a meaningful way within your school context.

Depending on the way in which your school works, you may also have access to training programmes offered within the local authority and by national bodies. These may include training in specific subject areas (including coaching awards), in teaching approaches (e.g. using ICT or creativity), in assessment or in aspects of classroom management (e.g. behaviour management). Again, you should use the targets set with your mentor for the induction period to identify which courses may be of most benefit.

If you decide that more formalized, academic study will best suit your needs then there are a number of options available to you. In order to explain these we need to return to the national Framework for Higher Education Qualifications (FHEQ).

In higher education there are a number of stages: the Postgraduate Certificate, the Postgraduate Diploma and Masters, all of which are level 7, and Doctorates which are at level 8. In theory, you could enrol on a Masters award, complete 60 credit points and then withdraw, taking with you a Postgraduate Certificate, although the extent to which this is possible varies from institution to institution. However, you have already reached this stage and therefore could be one-third of the way to a Masters award.

You do not necessarily need to complete a Masters award before moving on to Doctorate level. Some institutions allow you to enrol on the higher award with the proviso that you upgrade from Masters to Doctorate level at a time mutually agreed between yourself and your tutor. This upgrade requires you to demonstrate that you are capable of study at the higher level and that you have already undertaken work which can be developed appropriately.

What part of my PGCE at M-level can I use to transfer into a Masters award?

Although the Framework for Higher Education Qualifications (FHEQ) does not specify the number of credits required for each award stage, a Masters award is generally considered to be 180 credit points. These can be achieved through a completely modular structure, or through 120 credit points of modules and a dissertation worth 60 credit points. Therefore, if you have gained 60 credit points in your PGCE, this could constitute one-third of a Masters qualification. The details of the numbers of credits and the award to which you can transfer them vary, but there is little doubt that the changes in the FHEQ have impacted not just on PGCEs but also on the awards above these, and this has resulted in greater choice.

As a result of the Credit Accumulation Transfer Scheme, you will be able to apply for Accreditation of Prior Learning/Qualifications using your PGCE credits to most institutions, although there are still some who do not accept credits from another institution. The number of credits you can transfer does vary between institutions, although the position statements by many institutions indicate that they will accept up to 60 credit points as part of the study for a Masters award. Some will only accept M-level credits at level 7, while others will accept 30 credits at level 7 and 30 at level 6. This means that even though you may not gain Masters level in all your PGCE assignments, you may still be able to use the credit points to transfer into a Masters award at some institutions.

It will be important for you to consider how your PGCE programme outcomes map on to the Masters programme you are considering. Some institutions accept your PGCE credits without question, although others will want to see whether the outcomes from your PGCE modules match any of the modules in the Masters award you wish to transfer into. For example, if you wanted to apply for an MSc, you would have to demonstrate that your PGCE work had a specific science focus which, in combination with further modules, would enable you to meet the overall outcomes of the MSc award. It is likely that you will encounter greater difficulties in attempting to transfer to a more specialized, subject-specific Masters award, particularly if you have completed a primary PGCE, than if you transfer into a more generic education-based Masters award. For this reason, many institutions have revisited their Masters awards to ensure that the outcomes map on to their PGCE programmes.

It is also noteworthy that some institutions will ask you to 'hand back' your PGCE if you wish to use the credits as part of a Masters award. This is due to the notion of 'double counting', that is the idea that you are using the same credit points for two different awards – the PGCE and the Masters. If they do this, you are not allowed to list your PGCE on your curriculum vitae, apart from to indicate that you have gained QTS.

What course should I choose?

As a result of institutions revisiting their awards following changes to the FHEQ, a range of awards are now available which articulate well with the PGCE. These include generic Masters awards in such areas as teaching, education, educational studies and practitioner research, and more specific routes such as early years, science, mathematics, technology and special educational needs. The award you will exit with also varies widely from institution to institution and include:

- Master of Arts in Education (MAEd)

- Master of Education (MEd)

- Master in Education (MEd)

- Master of Philosophy (MPhil)

- Master of Science (MSc)

- Master in Research (MRes)

- Master of Teaching (MTeach)

Choosing the best route for you can be a daunting prospect but reflecting on what you want out of Masters study is always a good place to start.

Consider your own aspirations. What do you want a Masters degree to do for you personally and professionally? There is no fixed answer to which route you should follow but, as a general rule of thumb, the EdD, MTeach, MEd and MAEd routes tend to be more practice-based, the DPhil and MRes more research-based while the MSc. routes tend to be more specifically linked to subjects which are more scientific or technological in nature. Some routes will allow you to transfer in your PGCE M-level credits as they fit the overall programme learning outcomes whereas others are more difficult to assimilate. In general, the more generic routes will be available to most PGCE graduates.

You may also decide that you prefer to go straight to doctorate level. In most cases doctorate awards will have a staged exit point at Masters with the two most common routes being Doctor of Philosophy (DPhil), with a staged exit route of Masters in Philosophy (MPhil), or Doctor of Education (EdD) with a staged exit route of Master of Education (MEd).

Whatever route you are considering, my advice is threefold. First choose something that you are interested in. It is likely that you will be pursuing this award part-time and therefore the subject and structure of the programme will need to keep you motivated. For example, some students prefer a more modular approach to studying as the expectation of regularly submitted work provides set timeframes and imposes a structure while others prefer a more open structure which only has one or two points of submission. Secondly, your area of study should support your personal and professional aspirations. For example, if you intend to progress along a subject leadership role, you may decide it would be best to pursue a subject focus route. Thirdly, choose something which enables you to continue to develop your understanding of the relationship between theory, research and practice, in other words something which articulates well with your current employment. For example, my Masters was undertaken when I was a cross-phase advisory teacher for science. At this time I was involved in a funded project which looked at effective transfer in science from Key Stage 2 to Key Stage 3. My role was to research the perceptions of pupils both in terms of their understanding of science in each phase and in terms of their thinking about the strategies employed by both phases to support curricular continuity and progression. This work became the basis for my dissertation, 'Moving to the BIG school', and enabled me to complete my Masters alongside my current role.

Activity

Using the areas for development identified on your CEDP is often a good starting point as you would need to explore these further anyway. Choose one of these areas and identify one piece of research and one theory which you could use to develop your practice. Ask your mentor if you can observe him/her teaching and focus on the area you want to develop. Now see if you can use the theory, research, practice model discussed in Chapter 1 to develop your own practice in one key way. (Look at the case study of Karen outlined in Chapter 5 to help refine your thinking.) Evaluate the effect of this and then begin the cycle again. Could this be the start of your further study?

Once you have an idea about the type of study you would like to do for your Masters, look at the programme specifications from the institutions you are considering. You may find the following questions useful:

- Do the learning outcomes for the programme build on your PGCE and do they match your personal and professional aspirations?

- How is the programme structured and organized (modular, dissertation, etc.) and does this suit your way of working? Think here about how good you are at organizing your time and meeting deadlines. If you are not very good at this then a more structured, modular approach may suit you better than an open approach which requires you to set your own deadlines.

- To what extent is the programme taught and how much would you be expected to do independently?

- What level of support can you expect to receive from your supervising tutor?

- What qualifications/experience/interest do the tutors have in your anticipated field of study?

- What assessment strategies are used to evaluate your work? Do you prefer a modular structure with regular assignments or a more open structure which allows you to set your own timescales with a fixed end point for submission?

- What fees are associated with the programme and how will these be paid?

- What time limits does the institution impose in terms of transferring in your credits from your PGCE and in completing the final award?

When should I continue with my studies?

For many beginning teachers, getting through the induction year is their main priority; beginning a Masters course is relegated to the years beyond this. It is true that the induction year is demanding, and you will need time to settle into your new role, but this is also a time when the relationship between theory, research and practice is very fresh in your mind, and therefore it may be good to capitalize on this by formalizing it through focused study. You may be convinced that you will have no time to study as well as teach, but just consider for a moment what you have been doing over the past year. You have learnt (hopefully!) how to organize your time effectively and how to balance the practicalities of everyday life with higher-order thinking. Surely this is a good time to continue to evolve your skills in this rather than waiting a year, when some of the academic skills may not come back quite so easily?

Doing your induction year should not be a reason for not doing a Masters programme. Choosing a Masters programme which will support your current development is a real strength and many institutions have recognized this by developing M-level modules which can be done independently and build up to a Masters award as you progress. For example, you could complete a module which capitalizes on your Newly Qualified Teacher status in your first year of teaching but then do nothing else until later the following year. If you choose to adopt this more modular approach, however, do check the time limit for completion of the award imposed by the institution you are enrolling with.

When considering when to pursue further study, find out what 'currency' the institution where you intend to do your Masters holds. For example, some institutions will allow you to transfer M-level credits gained within the last five years while others only allow those gained within the last three years. This should not prevent you doing a Masters at these institutions but you will not be able to use your PGCE credits as part of this.

Potential barriers to further study

When deciding whether to continue your studies you will need to take into account the potential barriers. Time, workload, support from family, colleagues and your school, financial constraints, professional needs during induction and access are often identified as key constraints to further study. Although these may seem to present insurmountable difficulties, you may find that each can be overcome with careful planning and thought.

Time is the most commonly stated reason for not continuing with academic study, and to be fair this can be problematic. Teaching is tiring and can become all-consuming, particularly in your first year. However, it is important to maintain an appropriate work–life balance and you should continue to have social time with friends and family and time for yourself throughout your teaching career. If you choose your study focus carefully, studying can become a very rewarding part of 'your time'. Think about how you spend your time at present and draw up a weekly plan listing all the things you *have* to do (working, shopping, ironing, cleaning, ferrying children about), and all the things you *like* to do (socializing with friends, going out as a family, playing sport, attending an evening class).

Now think about how much time you spend doing 'work avoidance' tasks. I can spend hours tidying my wardrobe or gardening when I am supposed to be meeting a deadline! Are there ways in which you can work 'smarter' by combining tasks or doing them slightly differently? Can you involve the family by delegating some of your tasks, such as tidying the children's bedrooms, sorting out washing or doing the shopping? If you can achieve this, then you will be able to make space for further study, if you cannot, then it is not the time to pursue this.

In terms of workload, look carefully at the reasons why this is so heavy. Are you still struggling with planning and preparing resources, and if so, why? Is it because you find these difficult or are you planning each lesson from scratch rather than using the planning and resources available? We all strive for perfection in our teaching but the nature of teaching and the challenges you face mean that you will rarely feel that you achieve it. You therefore need to identify a realistic timescale for your planning and preparation and stick to it. If you have been given too much responsibility in your teaching, talk to your mentor or your head teacher and work out ways in which this burden can be eased. There is no weakness in admitting that you are over-burdened: a good school will want to support you in reaching your full potential and should be willing to work with you in order to support this.

Support from family members is essential. Explain to them why it is important to you to continue to study so that they understand your motivation. Work out with them how you can achieve this as a family and involve friends in possible solutions. Children can be very resentful of parents who are busy studying or working all the time, particularly if you were at home full-time before, so explain how you will manage your schedule so that they get time with you, and involve them in tasks around the house so that they can support you. A friend of mine has recently got her two children doing the weekly shopping online. They have a budget to stick to and if they manage to get all the weekly shop within this they can have the remaining money to spend for themselves!

Try to interest your colleagues in what you are doing, not by becoming the staffroom bore but by demonstrating the ways in which your study may support both your own and their practice. For example, doing a module on science may result in you being able to prepare teaching resources for other colleagues as well as yourself, and may result in them returning the favour in other curriculum areas that you find more challenging.

It is likely that you will be paying off your student loans in your first few years of teaching and therefore the additional financial burden of further study may not be an option. However, look at this as a long-term aim. Having a Masters will probably support any career aspirations you may have so has future potential in improving your financial position. In the short term, consider enrolling for a modular Masters, which allows you to enrol on and pay for one module at a time. This means you can complete the modules at your own pace and not get locked into a programme which requires you to complete within a given timeframe. If you are very lucky you may even be able to persuade your school to pay part or all of the costs if they can see the benefits to the school. Some local authorities have negotiated free modules with local institutions, particularly in the area of induction modules. The institution hopes you will then continue to study there and some receive financial support from the Training and Development Agency for Schools to subsidize in-service teacher training.

Your professional needs during induction should underpin your choice of Masters programme. Something which complements what you are already doing is preferable to something which adds another level of work to your already busy year. Induction modules are a particularly good way of achieving this.

Access to an institution of your choice may be an issue. Investigate whether they have any distance learning or online modules, or if they teach modules in intensive periods, perhaps over weekends, rather than requiring you to attend each week. Some institutions also offer out-stations which bring the teaching to your local teachers' centre or a local school rather than expecting you to travel to the institution.

 Activity

Divide a piece of A4 paper into two columns, and head one 'Barriers' and the other 'Solutions'. In the first column, list the barriers that may prevent you continuing your studies, and then in the second column see if you can identify potential solutions. Try to think of more than one solution if you can, in case one proves unfeasible.

There is no doubt that if you want to pursue further study, potential barriers can be overcome. Equally it is very important that you really want to do it in the first place. If having listed the reasons why you should not do it you find yourself unable to think of any solutions, then it is likely that this is not the right time for you to consider it.

Summary

Successfully completing the PGCE M-level should provide you with the confidence to continue your studies, and there can be little doubt that this is a good way of ensuring you continue to develop both personally and professionally.

Hopefully this chapter has identified some of the options available to you and enabled you to find solutions to potential barriers to continuing your studies. You may find the following questions helpful when considering your next step.

LIBRARY, UNIVERSITY OF CHESTER

- What areas for development have you identified in your Career Entry Development Profile and what opportunities are there for incorporating one of these areas into further academic study?

- What elements of M-level study did you enjoy, or not enjoy, and why?

- What elements of your own practice and that of others do you find interesting and what potential is there in pursuing further study in this area?

- Does your interest lie within your subject area or are you more interested in generic aspects of teaching and learning?

- What solutions are available to help you manage potential barriers to further study?

Further reading

Denby, N. et al. (2008) *Masters Level Study in Education: A Guide to Success*. Maidenhead: Open University Press. Covering aspects from writing a literature review to ethical working this book is useful reading for both the PGCE student and for those wishing to move into a Masters award.

Your local institution's website is also a good place to start looking for the routes on offer.

INDEX

TEACHING PRIMARY ENGLISH

Jackie Brien *University of Chester*

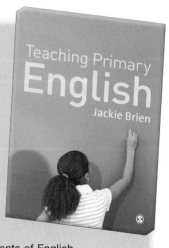

Literacy empowers learning across the whole curriculum and language is at the centre of all learning in primary education.

Aware of current curriculum developments and drawing from the latest research **Teaching Primary English** encourages teacher education students to develop a deeper understanding of the essential issues involved in teaching English in order to approach a career in the primary classroom with the confidence and knowledge required to succeed.

Taking a fresh approach to the main elements of teaching primary English, Jackie Brien strikes an engaging balance between the practical requirements of English teaching and encouraging informed reflection on key aspects of primary literacy.

Jackie Brien is Curriculum Leader for English, Communication, Language and Literacy at the University of Chester.

CONTENTS

What teachers of literacy know and do \ Speaking and listening \ Reading with and for understanding \ Teaching phonics for reading and writing \ Learning and teaching writing: the knowledge and processes of composing text \ Accuracy and presentation: the secretarial aspects of writing \ Inclusive learning and teaching of English \ Information and communication technologies in the teaching of English \ English and literacy beyond the classroom \ Planning to ensure progress in English \ Assessment and targeting in English

READERSHIP

Students studying primary English on primary initial teacher education courses including undergraduate, postgraduate and employment-based routes into teaching; also newly qualified teachers

December 2011 • 256 pages
Cloth (978-0-85702-156-4) • £60.00 / Paper (978-0-85702-157-1) • £19.99

ALSO FROM SAGE

TEACHING CHILDREN 3 – 11

A Student's Guide

Third Edition

Edited by **Anne D Cockburn** *University of East Anglia* and **Graham Handscomb** *Essex County Council*

Focusing on the major topics underpinning professional studies strands in primary and early years teacher education, Teaching Children 3-11 provides indispensable coverage of vital practical and conceptual issues that support good teaching practice. This third edition of the popular textbook has been carefully revised following detailed lecturer feedback to meet the evolving needs of students training to teach across the 3-11 age range.

Featuring four new chapters on curriculum development, cross-curricular teaching, diversity and inclusion, and communication in the classroom, and engaging with the growing need for Masters-level study in teacher education, the new edition offers a balanced contemporary overview of modern teaching practice in an engaging and accessible manner.

This is essential reading for all students on primary and early years initial teacher education courses including undergraduate (BEd, BA with QTS), postgraduate (PGCE, SCITT), and employment-based routes into teaching. It will also be invaluable for those starting out on their professional careers.

CONTENTS

November 2011 • 368 pages
Cloth (978-0-85702-486-2) • £70.00 / Paper (978-085702-487-9) • £23.99

ALSO AVAILABLE FROM SAGE

THE PRIMARY CURRICULUM

A Creative Approach

Edited by **Patricia Driscoll** *Canterbury Christ Church University*, **Andrew Lambirth** *University of Greenwich* and **Judith Roden** *Canterbury Christ Church University*

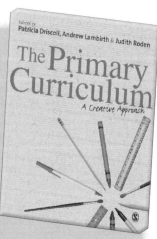

Providing an overview of the knowledge, skills and understanding needed to teach the primary curriculum, this book offers an informed critical approach to the teaching of core and foundation subjects in primary education.

Underpinned by contemporary research and current policy **The Primary Curriculum** combines coverage of key subject-specific issues with relevant pedagogical approaches to teaching, offering a comprehensive overview of each major subject of primary education.

Particular emphasis is placed on cross-curricular and creative approaches to teaching intelligently across different subject areas within the current curriculum framework. Curriculum progression from Foundation Stage through to Key Stage 2 is also emphasised.

The Primary Curriculum is an essential companion for all students on primary initial teacher education courses.

CONTENTS

Andrew Lambirth An Introduction to Literacy \ **Gina Donaldson** An Introduction to Mathematics \ **Judith Roden** An Introduction to Science \ **James Archer** An Introduction to Design Technology \ **Rosemary Walters** An Introduction to History \ **Simon Hoult** An Introduction to Geography \ **Kristy Howells** An Introduction to Physical Education \ **Michael Green An Introduction to Information Communication Technology** \ **Vanessa Young** An Introduction to Music \ **Claire Hewlett and Claire Unsworth** An Introduction to Art and Design \ **Lynn Revell** An Introduction to Religious Education \ **Patricia Driscoll** An Introduction to Primary Languages \ **Jonathan Barnes** An Introduction to Cross-Curricular Learning

READERSHIP

All students on primary initial teacher education courses including undergraduate (BEd, BA with QTS), postgraduate (PGCE, SCITT), and employment-based routes into teaching

August 2011 • 288 pages
Cloth (978-1-84920-596-2) • £65.00 / Paper (978-1-84920-597-9) • £22.99

ALSO FROM SAGE